Nathan Augustus Cobb

Nematodes, Mostly Australian and Fijian

Nathan Augustus Cobb

Nematodes, Mostly Australian and Fijian

ISBN/EAN: 9783337315146

Printed in Europe, USA, Canada, Australia, Japan

Cover: Foto ©ninafisch / pixelio.de

More available books at **www.hansebooks.com**

DEPARTMENT OF AGRICULTURE,

NEW SOUTH WALES.

MISCELLANEOUS PUBLICATIONS, No.

NEMATODES, MOSTLY AUSTRALIAN AND FIJIAN,

BY

N. A. COBB.

Reprinted from the *Macleay Memorial Volume*, by arrangement with the Linnean Society of New South Wales.

————◦———

Sydney :
F. CUNNINGHAME & CO., PRINTERS, 146 PITT STREET
1893

DEPARTMENT OF AGRICULTURE,

NEW SOUTH WALES.

MISCELLANEOUS PUBLICATIONS, No. 13.

NEMATODES, MOSTLY AUSTRALIAN AND FIJIAN.

BY

N. A. COBB.

Reprinted from the *Macleay Memorial Volume*, by arrangement with the Linnean Society of New South Wales.

Sydney:
F. CUNNINGHAME & CO., PRINTERS, 146 PITT STREET.
1893

NEMATODES, MOSTLY AUSTRALIAN AND FIJIAN.

By N. A. Cobb.

(Plates I.-VII.)

INTRODUCTORY NOTE.

The following pages contain descriptions, accompanied by about one hundred and seventy figures, of eighty-two species of Nematodes, of which about half have not been hitherto described. In a number of cases the anatomical details have been worked out in a manner worthy the attention of the morphologist.

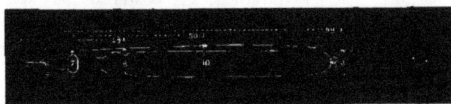

Fig. 1.—Diagram in explanation of the descriptive formula used for Nematode worms ; 6, 7, 8, 10, 6 are the transverse measurements, while 7, 14, 28, 50, 88 are the corresponding longitudinal measurements. The formula in this case is :—

$$\frac{7\cdot\ \ 14\cdot\ \ 28\cdot\ \ 50\cdot\ \ 88\cdot}{6\cdot\ \ 7\cdot\ \ 8\cdot\ \ 10\cdot\ \ 6\cdot}$$

The unit of measurement is the hundredth part of the length of the worm, whatever that may be. The measurements become, therefore, percentages of the length.

The measurements are taken with the animal viewed in profile ; the first is taken at the base of the pharynx, the second at the nerve-ring, the third at the cardiac constriction, the fourth at the vulva in females and at the middle (M) in males, the fifth at the anus.

GENUS MONONCHUS, Bastian.

The genus *Mononchus* is composed of herbivorous free-living Nematodes, not marine, having the average formulæ $\frac{2\cdot5\ \ 7\cdot6\ \ 25\cdot\ \ \cdot60'\ \ 90\cdot}{\cdot5\ \ 2\cdot8\ \ 3\cdot6\ \ 3\cdot8\ \ 2\cdot}$ 2mm. and $\frac{2\cdot5\ \ 7\cdot6\ \ 25\cdot\ \ -M-\ \ 90\cdot}{\cdot5\ \ 2\cdot8\ \ 3\cdot6\ \ 3\cdot8\ \ 2\cdot}$ 2·(—)mm. They are readily recognised by their capacious pharynx, containing from one to three commonly conspicuous teeth, whose function is, in conjunction with certain minute file-like or rasp-like areas on the wall of the pharynx, to masticate the food, which consists of fresh and succulent vegetable matter, such as rootlets, or the tissues of aquatic or sub-aquatic plants, or the protected tissues found among the sheaths of the leaves of certain land-plants. The thick transparent cuticle of these worms is destitute both of hairs and striæ. The neck is sometimes almost cylindrical, but is usually conoid, and invariably ends in a truncate head, which in one species

(Tunbridgensis) is contracted, but in all the others is slightly expanded at the lip-region. Two rows of tactile organs, each consisting of six conical innervated papillæ, surround the mouth,—the outer spreading row being situated on the margin of the head, while the inner row closely surrounds the mouth. These papillæ are usually of uniform size, but sometimes those of one row, usually the inner, are larger than those of the other. It is tolerably certain that the number of lips is three, and that each lip is two-parted, though this is not an easy thing to demonstrate, owing to the fact that the lips are very low and nearly confluent. The mouth-opening is small, the length of the passage leading from it to the pharynx being determined by the thickness of the lips, which are uncommonly bulky and powerful. Behind the lips the pharynx assumes at once its full width, which is tolerably uniform throughout its length in most species; in a few, however, the posterior part narrows somewhat gradually instead of suddenly. The absolute length of the pharynx varies, speaking roughly, from 30μ to 60μ, the smaller species, as a rule, possessing a smaller pharynx, but not by any means proportionately smaller. *M. digiturus*, for instance, notwithstanding that it is only half as large as *M. longicaudatus*, has a pharynx quite as large as that of the latter. In form the pharynx varies between triquetrous and hexagonal, usually three and sometimes all of its edges being clearly indicated by longitudinal more or less curved chitinous ribs. A dorsal tooth seems always to be present, though it is occasionally inconspicuous. It is usually situated near the middle of the dorsal side of the pharyngeal cavity and projects forward and inward, often so much as to be very conspicuous. A few species possess ventral submedian teeth, rivalling the dorsal in size, and placed on a par with it; probably these submedian teeth exist in a more or less rudimentary condition in most of the species, but have been overlooked and hence left unnoticed by the authors. Portions of the chitinous walls of the pharynx are covered with minute teeth or roughnesses, resembling sometimes those of a rasp (first noticed by Dujardin) and sometimes those of a mill-saw file (first noticed by Bütschli). These rasp-like or file-like roughnesses appear to have a definite relation to the form of the pharynx, and to have a definite function, namely, to aid in mastication. I have observed that the species possessing rasp-like roughnesses have them placed in opposition to the projecting part of the dorsal tooth, the areas covered by the minute teeth beginning near the lateral lines and extending toward the ventral part of the pharynx, where the teeth seem less developed than at the sides; the dorsal surface of the pharynx near the dorsal tooth is quite smooth. The species observed by me possessing plain transverse striations resembling the teeth of a mill-saw file, are species in which the dorsal tooth is rudimentary and situated near the base of the pharynx, the position of the striations, however, being precisely that of the above-described bands of rasp-like teeth; the walls of the pharynx are, moreover, in this case traversed by certain curved transverse ridges of such a complicated nature that even after considerable study of them I can

only assert that they must impart to the wall of the pharynx an irregular sculpturing, doubtless well adapting it for mastication, for which purpose the exterior of the pharynx seems supplied with more abundant and more powerful muscles than in the other species. Doubtless these differences can be made the basis of a division of the genus into two natural subgenera. In those cases where the dorsal tooth is placed in the neighbourhood of the lips, I have observed that the anterior walls of the pharynx, or the internal surface of the lips, are armed with large somewhat tooth-like almost backward-pointing processes, which I judge from their position (I have never seen them act) to be the antagonistics of the dorsal tooth. The lips and walls of the pharynx are always supplied with numerous and powerful muscles, concerning whose action Bütschli remarked that the head was often seen to contract longitudinally.

The œsophagus is very simple, being a tube half to two-thirds as wide as the neck, wider posteriorly than anteriorly, without bulbs of any sort, and separated from the intestine by a distinct but shallow constriction, which is sometimes double owing to the fact that the intestine is joined closely to the cardia for a short distance and then suddenly expands. The intestine is two-thirds to three-fourths as wide as the body and ends in a short and narrow rectum, only about two-thirds as long as the anal body-diameter. The intestine is usually thin-walled and is composed of cells whose granules are arranged so as to give rise to a tessellation, often of such a perfect and beautiful kind as to render these worms a most attractive spectacle. The nerve-ring surrounds the œsophagus squarely near the division between its anterior and middle third; before and behind the ring the usual ganglion cells occur. All the species are eyeless. The lateral fields are well developed, being one-fifth to one-third as wide as the body. The lateral organs have remained until now undiscovered in all the species; I find, however, that in *longicaudatus* they exist opposite the middle of the pharynx in the form of small transverse ellipsoidal openings. The ventral gland, too, has hitherto remained unseen, but in *megalaimus* and *digiturus* a pore exists just behind the nerve-ring, and this pore has every appearance of being the outlet of the ventral gland.

The tail varies in length from one-fiftieth to one-fifth of the length of the animal; when short it is conoid, and when long it is conoid in the anterior part and narrow and cylindroid in the remaining part, being always slightly swollen at the terminus, which is rounded and gives exit to the secretions of the caudal glands, probably always three in number.

In two species (*digiturus* and *gymnolaimus*) the female sexual apparatus is single, in all the others as yet made known it is double, the two parts being symmetrically reflexed, in spite of which fact, however, the projecting vulva is usually situated near the beginning of the posterior third of the body, a position in harmony with the unusually great length of the œsophagus, which seldom occupies in adults less than one-fourth the length of the body. The eggs are usually ellipsoidal and somewhat longer than the body is wide; they are generally deposited before segmentation begins. The reflexed part of the ovaries is usually short, seldom reaching more than half-way back to the vulva.

The tail end of the male generally resembles that of his mate in form, but differs in the presence of numerous low broad papillæ, of which a ventral row of a dozen or more closely approximated ones are found in front of the anus, while several others are found scattered over the tail. Each of the two equal slender spicula is generally supplied near the middle of the shaft with an additional piece of chitin which doubtless serves to render it less flexible. The accessory piece is double and surrounds the spicula.

While the genus *Mononchus* is one easily recognised and defined, it is one whose affinities have been somewhat misunderstood. It does not stand in such close relationship to *Oncholaimus* as was formerly supposed. The structure of the pharynx which was thought to give it that relationship is now more clearly understood, and is seen to present a superficial rather than a real resemblance to the pharynx of *Oncholaimus*. The structure of the lips is very different in the two genera, those of *Mononchus* being thick, armed with a double row of prominent papillæ and not accompanied by cephalic setæ, while those of *Oncholaimus* are thin, lack at any rate conspicuous papillæ and are always accompanied by setæ. The inner walls of the pharyngeal cavity of *Mononchus* are moreover armed with rasp-like or file-like roughnesses, not seen in *Oncholaimus*. Leaving the pharynx we come to other very striking differences. For instance, no ventral gland has yet been demonstrated in *Mononchus*, although it probably exists, while it is never absent and is usually conspicuous in *Oncholaimus*; then, too, the nerve-ring in the former genus is always considerably in front of the middle of the œsophagus, while in the latter it is near the middle or behind it; again the male copulatory organs of the two genera differ widely from each other, and this brings to mind another difference, namely, the extreme rarity of males in one case and the comparative abundance in the other; *Oncholaimus* is marine, while *Mononchus* lives in soils and on the surface of land plants; the peculiar organ seen in the females of *Oncholaimus* has not been met with in *Mononchus*. These differences and others seem to me to show that only a somewhat remote relationship exists between these two genera.

I am of opinion that the worms belonging to this genus can by no means be termed harmless to vegetation. My opinion is based on data collected during several years and is therefore worthy of the attention of vegetable pathologists.

Mononchus is distributed all over the world. I have myself examined specimens from North America, Europe, tropical Asia, Australia and Fiji. The species do not so far as I have observed differ widely from one another, though this statement may be qualified by our lack of knowledge concerning the males. They are universally found congregated about the roots of plants or in the axils of their leaves, where they thrive by gnawing at the epidermis and the subjacent cells. There can be no doubt that they sometimes occur in sufficient numbers to do visible injury, as witness the following observations :

The edible part of three bunches of nice-looking celery bought of a Chinaman in Sydney was cut off as far up as it was tender,—nearly to the first leaflets. It was washed by hand in a tin dish in tank water, free from nematodes. The washings gave about 200-300 nematodes as follows.

    1. *Mononchus longicaudatus*, Cobb, very abundant ;

    2. *Rhabditis* sp.? less abundant ;

    3. *Plectus parietinus*, Bast., in numbers equalling the last ;

    4. *Diplogaster trichuris*, Cobb, a few ;

    5. *Mononchus* sp.? few ;

    6. *Dorylaimus* sp.? two at least.

The leaves were also washed ; one nematode, a *Mononchus*, was found.

These observations lead me to believe that the damage these worms are capable of doing to plants, especially young seedlings, is considerable, though there is as yet a dearth of evidence on that point.

Key.

Female sexual organ single: Cheeks thin, i.e., pharynx one-half as wide as the head , teeth basal—

Armed with three equal teeth	1. *digiturus.*
Armed with a single small tooth	2. *gymnolaimus.*

Female sexual organs double : Cheeks thick, i.e., pharynx less than one-half as wide as the head ; dorsal tooth if present, central.

Length not much above half a millimetre.	3. *crassiusculus.*
Length at least one millimetre.	
Head contracted opposite the pharynx.	4. *Tunbridgensis.*
Head not so contracted.	
Dorsal tooth opposed by two large ventral submedian ones	5. *tridentatus.*
Dorsal tooth not opposed by others of any size.	
Tail conoid and ventrally arcuate.	
Anus at 98 %	6. *brachyurus.*

Anus at 96 % to 87 %.
    Worm about 1·mm. long.
        Pharynx thrice as long as wide...................... 7. *parvus.*
        Pharynx twice as long as wide...................... 8. *cristatus.*
        Pharynx about as long as wide..................... 9. *minor.*
    Worm about 1·8 mm. long.
        Pharynx narrow, twice as long as wide.......... 10. *papillatus.*
        Pharynx about as wide as long....... .... 11. *muscorum.*
    Worm about 3 mm. long .... 12. *major.*
Tail in the posterior part cylindroid.
    Anus at 82 %; pharynx less than three times as wide as long 13. *longicaudatus.*
    Anus at 86 %; pharynx four times as wide as long.......... 14. *truncatus.*
    Anus situated at length at not less than 90 %... .... { 15. *macrostoma.* / 16. *fovearum.*

1. **M. digiturus**, n.sp. $\frac{3.3 \quad 8.2 \quad 25.6 \quad 70^{12} \quad 92.}{2.6 \quad 3. \quad 3.4 \quad 3.4 \quad 2.3}$ 1·4 mm. The truncate head is only very slightly expanded. Each lateral field appears to end in a curve opposite the anterior part of the pharynx, and I surmise that these curves are the lateral organs. The pharynx, which is as long as the head is wide and two-thirds as wide as long, is entered through a vestibule one-fifth as long as the pharynx proper ; three longitudinal chitinous ribs occur at the angles of the internal surface of the pharynx and near their bases are seen three subequal rather rudimentary basal teeth, of nearly equal size, only one-third as long as the cavity. The œsophagus is about three-fifths as wide as the neck, being in the middle somewhat narrower than elsewhere ; it is separated from the intestine by a distinct constriction. The gut is three-fourths as wide as the body and ends in a rectum a trifle longer than the anal body-diameter. A ventral pore occurs just behind the nerve-ring. The tail is arcuate-conoid to the somewhat blunt terminus. This and the next are the only known species in which the female sexual organs are not double and symmetrical, and as usual it is the posterior branch which has disappeared ; the remaining anterior branch is short and reflexed. The vulva is not prominent. Drawings are given on Pl. i.

This worm was found in small numbers about the roots of banana plants, Fiji, July, 1891. No males were seen.

2. **M. gymnolaimus**, n.sp. $\frac{2.6 \quad 6.8 \quad 23.5 \quad 07^{15} \quad 86.}{1.2 \quad 2.2 \quad 2.7 \quad 2.5 \quad 1.4}$ 2·94 mm. The neck of this species is cylindroid. The diameter of the inner circle of cephalic papillæ is half that of the outer circle. The vestibule is one-fourth as long as the pharynx proper. Opposite the anterior part of the pharynx, near what appears to be the termination of the lateral fields, occur small transverse elliptical markings, probably representing the lateral organs. The strongly three-ribbed triquetrous pharynx is as long as the head is wide, and one-half as wide as long, and presents a single rudimentary dorsal tooth at the base. The transverse striæ on the wall of the pharynx near the middle are

1μ apart. The intestine is laid close on to the cardia,—thus giving rise to a double constriction in the cardiac region,—and is composed of cells of such a size that twelve side by side make up its circumference. The concave-conoid rectum equals the anal body-diameter in length. What had every appearance of being the excretory pore occurred immediately behind the nerve-ring of every one of the numerous specimens examined. The lateral fields appear to be one-fifth as wide as the body. The tail is conoid to the terminus, which has a diameter one-seventh as great as the anal body-diameter. The vulva is not prominent. The uterus is as long as the reflexed part of the ovary, which reaches two-fifths the way back to the vulva. The ova are arranged single file. This worm is well drawn on Pl. I.

Hab.—Found in soil about the roots of banana plants, Fiji. No males were seen.

3. **M. crassiusculus,** Dujardin. $\frac{?\ ?\ 18\cdot6\ 66\cdot\ 80\cdot}{?\ ?\ ?\ 43\ ?}$ $\cdot$6 mm. This seems to be a doubtful or insufficiently-described species.

Hab.—France.

4. **M. Tunbridgensis,** Bastian. $\frac{3\cdot\ ?\ 23\cdot\ 50+\ 89\cdot}{3\cdot4\ ?\ 54\ 55\ 3\cdot2}$ 1·1 mm. This species is well characterised by the head diminishing in size opposite the base of the pharynx.

Hab.—Tunbridge, England.

5. **M. tridentatus,** de Man. $\frac{3\cdot\ 6\cdot5\ 24\cdot\ \cdot62\ ^{30}\ 89\cdot}{2\cdot1\ 2\cdot6\ 3\cdot\ 3\cdot1\ 1\cdot6}$ 3·2 mm. As its name indicates, this species possesses three teeth; they are of equal size, their apices being situated somewhat in front of the middle of the triquetrous pharynx. The œsophagus gradually widens posteriorly. The intestine, which is two-thirds as wide as the body, is separated from the œsophagus by a transparent cardiac region. The rectum is three-fourths as long as the anal body-diameter. The tail is conoid in both sexes. $\frac{2\cdot\ 6\cdot6\ 22\cdot\ M\ 91\cdot}{2\cdot1\ 2\cdot6\ 3\cdot\ 2\cdot1\ 2\cdot}$ 2·7 mm. The male has a ventral row of fifteen to seventeen papillæ in front of the anus, and presents also both dorsal and ventral papillæ on the tail. Each of the two equal slender arcuate spicula has a median stiffening piece of chitin. The accessory piece is two-parted, dentate, and encloses the spicula. Oblique copulatory muscles appear to be present.

Hab.—Moist soil, Holland; not common.

6. **M. brachyurus,** Bütschli. $\frac{1\ 1\ 24\cdot\ \cdot62\cdot\ 97\cdot5}{1\ ?\ 1\ 3\cdot6\ ?}$ 1·6 mm. The nearly cylindrical neck of this active species is said to terminate in a truncate head bearing a *single* row of rather large papillæ. The beaker-shaped pharynx is one-third as wide as the head, and twice as long as wide. Rasp-like areas on the wall of the pharynx oppose the dorsal tooth. The tail is conoid, blunt and arcuate. Two ventral papillæ are found near the vulva, one in front of it and one behind it. The reflexed portions of the

B

ovaries are short. $\frac{7}{7}\frac{7}{7}\frac{M}{2\cdot7}\frac{97\cdot}{7}$ 1·7 mm.   The tail of the male resembles that of the female in form.   A ventral row of ten to eleven large papillæ occurs in front of the anus. Dorsal as well as ventral papillæ are found on the tail.   Each of the two equal arcuate spicula is stiffened by an extra central piece of horn.   The accessory piece is two-parted and surrounds the spicula.

Hab.—Soil in meadows, Western Europe ; common.

7. **M. parvus,** de Man. $\frac{3\cdot1}{4}\frac{6\cdot5}{3\cdot6}\frac{29\cdot}{4\cdot7}\frac{'63\cdot'}{6\cdot2}\frac{93\cdot}{3\cdot}$ 1·1 mm.   The conoid neck terminates in a head with an expanded lip-region bearing the usual two circles of papillæ of which the inner are the larger.   The pharynx is a little over one-third as wide as the head, the dorsal tooth being small and central.   There are two small submedian teeth at the base of the pharynx.   The intestine is two-thirds as wide as the body and ends in a rectum two-thirds as long as the anal body-diameter.   The reflexed ovaries reach three-fourths the way back to the vulva.

Hab.—This active species is common in sandy meadows, Holland.

8. **M. cristatus,** Bastian. $\frac{3\cdot}{3\cdot6}\frac{7}{7}\frac{29\cdot}{5\cdot4}\frac{'50'\cdot+}{5\cdot5}\frac{67\cdot}{3\cdot2}$ 1·1 mm.   The œsophagus is about half as thick as the neck.   The intestine is two-thirds as wide as the body and ends in a rectum two-thirds as long as the anal body-diameter.

Hab.—England.

9. **M. minor,** n.sp.   An immature female gave the formula $\frac{3\cdot2}{3\cdot1}\frac{10\cdot}{3\cdot7}\frac{30\cdot}{4\cdot3}\frac{60\cdot}{4\cdot3}\frac{95\cdot}{2\cdot7}$ 1·mm. The head is less truncate than usual.   What appear to be lateral organs occur opposite the anterior part of the pharynx.   This latter is pyriform, being broadest anteriorly and is approached through a narrow vestibule nearly one-third as long as itself.   The thumb-shaped dorsal tooth projects half way across the pharyngeal cavity somewhat above the middle, and is opposed by half-a-dozen transverse rows of rasp-like teeth one micromillimetre apart, the upper of these rows being opposite the apex of the tooth and the lower opposite its middle.   The intestine is three-fifths as wide as the body, and the rectum is nearly equal to the anal body-diameter in length. The lateral fields are one-third as wide as the body.   The terminus of the tail is one-third as wide as the base.   The anatomy of this worm is well set forth on Pl. I.

Hab.—In soil about banana plants, Fiji, 1891.

10. **M. papillatus,** Bastian. $\frac{2\cdot5}{2\cdot3}\frac{7}{7}\frac{23\cdot}{3\cdot6}\frac{'67'\cdot}{4\cdot}\frac{93\cdot}{2\cdot5}$ 1·5 to 2·5 mm.   The triquetrous pharynx is about one-third as wide as the head, and has the rather small dorsal tooth situated a little in front of the middle.   The intestine is two-thirds as wide as the body.

Hab.—Among moss and grass, Western Europe ; common.

11. **M. muscorum,** Dujardin. $\frac{2 \cdot \quad 9 \cdot \quad 24 \cdot \quad '65 \cdot^{82} \quad 94 \cdot}{8 \cdot 1 \quad 2 \cdot 7 \quad 3 \cdot 2 \quad 3 \cdot 6} \frac{}{1 \cdot 6}$ 25 to 3 mm. The small dorsal tooth is near the centre of the pharynx, which is nearly one-half as wide as the head. The somewhat conoid œsophagus is three-fourths as wide as the neck, and the intestine is three-fourths as wide as the body. The rectum equals the anal body-diameter in length. The tail diminishes somewhat more rapidly near the terminus. The reflexed ovaries, each containing about a dozen ova arranged single file, extend half-way back to the projecting vulva. The eggs are one and one-half times as long as the body is wide, and three-fifths as wide as long. The anterior sexual organ is somewhat the larger.

Hab.—Among moss, &c., Western Europe.

12. **M. major,** n.sp. $\frac{1 \cdot 6 \quad 6 \cdot \quad 19 \cdot \quad '65 \cdot^{25} \quad 95 \cdot}{1 \cdot 6 \quad 2 \cdot 2 \quad 2 \cdot 6 \quad 2 \cdot 9} \frac{}{1 \cdot 6}$ 34 mm. The conoid neck terminates anteriorly in a truncate head bearing two rows of papillæ arranged as usual. The lateral organs are small and are situated near the lips,—slightly further forward than the point of the dorsal tooth. The narrow mouth leads into a pharynx as long as the head is wide, and two-fifths as wide as long, pointed at the bottom and strongly lined with chitin. The tooth, which, though small, is conspicuous, is situated considerably in front of the middle of the pharynx. The lateral fields are one-fifth as wide as the body. The intestine, which is marked off from the œsophagus by a shallow but distinct constriction, is greenish in colour, and composed of rather small cells showing an indistinct tessellation; the rectum is equal in length to the anal body-diameter. The conoid tail is ventrally arcuate, and ends in a blunt terminus containing a spinneret of the usual form. The eggs are probably less than twice as long as wide. The reflexed ovaries reach about half-way back to the vulva. $\frac{1 \cdot 5 \quad 6 \cdot 6 \quad 19 \cdot \quad -M- \quad 95 \cdot}{1 \cdot 5 \quad 2 \cdot 5 \quad 2 \cdot 9 \quad 2 \cdot 2}$ 34 mm. The tail of the male somewhat resembles that of the female in general form, but is more strongly arcuate. The spicula are elongated, arcuate, tapering toward both ends, not cephalated, and twice as long as the anal body-diameter, and are situated close together; the accessory pieces are well developed, and surround the spicula behind the middle, their blunt proximal points appearing in front of the ventral contour of the spicula. The protruding-muscles of the spicula are attached to the body-wall near the middle of the tail. A ventral row of about twelve conspicuous innervated mammiform accessory organs occur in front of the anus, and extend over a space about twice as long as the tail; each organ is situated on the posterior side of a transverse chitinous ridge extending one-fourth the distance round the body. The anterior two or three and the posterior one of these organs are smaller than the others; they are equidistantly placed, except the posterior, which is removed somewhat from its fellows. Oblique copulatory muscles are found co-extensive with the accessory organs and the crenate ejaculatory duct. The testicles occupy the middle third of the body. There are two pairs of ventrally submedian papillæ, also

innervated, on the anterior third of the tail, the posterior pair being near the end of the anterior third and the other pair half-way between that point and the anus. There are other papillæ (?) faintly visible on the dorsal side of the tail and elsewhere.

Hab.—Roots of plants, damp soil, Moss Vale, New South Wales.

13. **M. longicaudatus**, n.sp. $\frac{2\cdot5}{2\cdot2}\frac{7\cdot}{2\cdot7}\frac{22\cdot}{32}\frac{\cdot52}{57}\frac{\cdot21}{1\cdot9}\frac{84\cdot}{}$ 1·4 to 1·9 mm. Behind the nerve-ring the neck is conoid; but anteriorly it becomes slightly convex-conoid. The small elliptical lateral organs are placed close behind the outer row of papillæ, their long diameter being placed transversely; when seen in profile they appear as slits from which a process is seen to pass inward and backward. The pharynx, which is three-fifths as wide as the head and three times as long as wide, bears a rather small dorsal tooth near the middle, and very inconspicuous rudimentary projections on the ventral side. The vestibule is shorter than usual. The œsophagus is three-fifths as wide as the neck, its lumen being conspicuous because of the thickness of the chitinous lining. The cardia is large and well developed, and the intestine, which is four-fifths as wide as the body, is composed of cells of such a size that about twelve are required to build up the circumference.

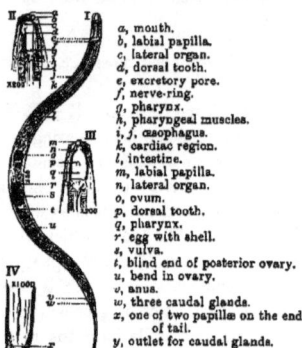

a, mouth.
b, labial papilla.
c, lateral organ.
d, dorsal tooth.
e, excretory pore.
f, nerve-ring.
g, pharynx.
h, pharyngeal muscles.
i, j, œsophagus.
k, cardiac region.
l, intestine.
m, labial papilla.
n, lateral organ.
o, ovum.
p, dorsal tooth.
q, pharynx.
r, egg with shell.
s, vulva.
t, blind end of posterior ovary.
u, bend in ovary.
v, anus.
w, three caudal glands.
x, one of two papillæ on the end of tail.
y, outlet for caudal glands.

FIG. 2.—I, female *Mononchus longicaudatus*; II, side view of head of same worm; III, ventral view of head of same worm; IV, end of tail of same worm.

The concave-conoid rectum is as long as the anal body-diameter. The lateral fields are one-seventh as wide as the body. The tail tapers most rapidly in the anterior half; posteriorly it is one-fifth as wide as at the anus. The reflexed ovaries extend half way back to the inconspicuous vulva and each contains fifteen to twenty eggs arranged about three abreast. The eggs are one and one-half times as long as the body is wide and one-half as wide as long. Segmentation appears to begin before the eggs are deposited,—at least in one case I observed an egg that had formed the first two blastomeres while yet in the uterus.

Hab.—Blanched part of celery, abundant, Sydney, N.S.W., Australia.

14. **M. truncatus**, Bastian. $\frac{2\cdot6}{3\cdot}\frac{7}{1}\frac{25\cdot}{6\cdot}\frac{50+}{5\cdot3}\frac{86\cdot}{3\cdot4}$ 1·76 mm. The elongated pharynx is one-third as wide as the head, the blunt dorsal tooth being situated near its middle. The intestine is three-fourths as wide as the body and the rectum is two-thirds as long as the anal body-diameter. Tail in the anterior two-thirds conoid, thence cylindrical and one-fourth as wide as at the anus. $\frac{2\cdot6}{7}\frac{7}{7}\frac{25\cdot}{7}\frac{M}{7}\frac{92\cdot}{7}$ 2·mm. The male tail

is more slender, the posterior two-thirds being cylindrical and only one-sixth as wide as at the anus. A ventral row of eighteen or nineteen equidistant papillæ or accessory organs is found just in front of the anus. The low post-anal papillæ are arranged as follows : 1, near the anus a pair of ventral submedian ; 2, near the other end of the anterior third of the tail another pair of ventral submedian ; 3, on the middle third of the tail three dorsal ; 4, on the terminus two. The two equal setaceous spicula are about half as long as the tail, their distal halves being arcuate and their proximæ cephalated by slight expansion. The two slender accessory pieces are parallel to the spicula and two-fifths as long.

Hab.—Among moss and aquatic plants, and in mud and sand near by, Western Europe.

15. **M. microstoma,** Bastian. $\frac{12}{26}\frac{7}{31}\frac{25}{34}\frac{\cdot 50}{34}\frac{90}{3}\cdot$ 2·5 mm. The labial papillæ of the inner row are the larger. The dorsal tooth is located a little in front of the middle of the elongated pharynx and is opposed by transverse chitinous ridges on the wall of the ventral side of the cavity. There are also small teeth at the base of the pharynx. The intestine is two-thirds as wide as the body and the rectum is one-half as long as the anal body-diameter. The anterior fourth of the tail is conoid ; thence it is very narrow to the slightly swollen terminus. The form of the male is similar to that of his mate. There is a ventral row of twenty pre-anal papillæ, and three ventral, as well as some lateral, post-anal ones. The slender spicula are bent at a blunt angle. The accessory piece is slender and much shorter than the spicula. Oblique copulatory muscles appear to be present.

Hab.—Fresh soil and fresh water, Holland, common ; England.

16. **M. fovearum,** Dujardin. $\frac{7}{7}\frac{7}{7}\frac{14\cdot8}{7}\frac{50\cdot}{3\cdot}\frac{95\cdot}{7}$ 2·5 mm. This species is insufficiently known.

Hab.—France.

Genus CHROMADORA, Bastian.

1. **C. minima,** n.sp. $\frac{2\cdot6}{12}\frac{11\cdot}{36}\frac{20\cdot}{43}\frac{43\cdot}{46}\frac{84\cdot}{32}$ 4 mm. is the formula found from the measurements of the only two specimens seen, both immature females. The cuticle is traversed by very fine transverse striæ resolvable with the highest powers of the microscope into rows of dots. The cylindroid neck is capped by a truncate head bearing on its outer margin six spreading setæ, each about one-sixth as long as the head is wide. The number of lips appears to be twelve, as indicated by the number of longitudinal ribs round the mouth opening. The spiral lateral organs are situated

a trifle behind the bottom of the pharynx ; each is a spiral one-fourth as wide as the neck, the right being a left-handed spiral of two turns, and the left being a similar right-handed spiral. The pharynx differs somewhat from that of the typical *Chromadora* as known to me, and this has led me to believe that it will soon be found necessary to re-group the species of this genus, and possibly to create new genera for the reception of some of them. Roughly speaking, the pharynx has the form of a triquetrous pyramid. The dorsal tooth is situated somewhat behind the middle of the pharynx, and when seen in profile appears to be arched over near its apex by a process above it. Opposite the dorsal tooth occurs a ventral projection somewhat resembling a rudimentary tooth inverted. The animal is so very small that these particulars can only be made out with high powers. There are no eyes. The œsophagus is one-half as wide as the neck and ends posteriorly in a spheroidal swelling two-thirds as wide as the neck. The cardiac constriction is very deep and conspicuous. The intestine is two-thirds as wide as the body, and its cells contain granules of various sizes. The conoid rectum somewhat exceeds the anal body-diameter in length. The anus is much depressed. The tail tapers very little, being one-half as wide at the apiculate terminus as at the base. Caudal glands are present. The vulva projects somewhat. Two sketches of this *Chromadora* are given on Pl. II.

Hab.—Soil about the roots of banana plants, Fiji, July, 1891.

C. Musæ, n.sp. $\frac{2\cdot4\quad 7\cdot\quad 17\cdot\quad 7\quad 86\cdot}{1\cdot6\quad 3\cdot3\quad 3\cdot5\quad 1\quad 2\cdot3}$ The cuticle has much the same structure as in *C. minima*. The cylindroid neck is surmounted by a rather truncate head bearing no setæ, or such that they escaped observation with very high powers. The spiral lateral organs are placed opposite the middle of the pharynx, each being one-fourth as wide as the head ; the right-hand organ is a left-handed spiral of two turns and the left-hand organ is a similar right-handed spiral. The approach to the pharynx is cyathiform and ribbed as is usual in this genus. The pharynx is somewhat irregularly elongated and the dorsal tooth small and so situated that its blunt apex is somewhat further back than the lateral organs. The œsophagus is slightly expanded to receive the pharynx, but through the greater portion of its length it is only one-third to one-half as wide as the neck ; posteriorly it expands to form a prolate bulb three-fourths as wide as the base of the neck. The nerve-ring is narrow and somewhat oblique. Nothing was seen of the ventral excretory organ or its pore. The intestine is two-thirds as wide as the body. The tail is conoid to the apiculate terminus. Three sketches of this worm, which is of about the same size as *C. minima*, are given on Pl. II.

Hab.—·Found in soil about the roots of banana plants, Fiji, July, 1891.

Genus DIPLOGASTER, Schultze.

The genus *Diplogaster* is composed of free-living forms, not marine, characterised by the possession of a large pharynx armed with one or more teeth, and an œsophagus with two well developed bulbs. If only one tooth is present it is dorsal; if more than one, then the larger may be dorsal and the others subsidiary, or more often all may be small and basal. The average dimensions are indicated by the following formulæ :— $\frac{1·6}{8·4} \frac{11·}{3·6} \frac{18·}{4·} \frac{·48^{23}}{4·} \frac{73·}{1·9}$ 1·11 mm. $\frac{1·6}{12·} \frac{10·9}{2·8} \frac{16·}{3·} \frac{·M^{37}}{3·} \frac{76·}{2·6}$ 1·mm The cuticle is commonly transversely striated, though apparently sometimes not, and moreover presents longitudinal striations or perhaps more properly speaking wings, sometimes to the number of forty, of which those on the lateral fields are usually more prominent, they being the only ones that continue far on the tail. Both these sorts of markings are often resolvable into rows of dots or circles. The only hairs thus far observed on the body are the cephalic setæ seen on a few species, and those on the male: these latter are doubtless tactile and partake more of the nature of papillæ than of ordinary hairs; their arrangement and grouping will presently be described. The papilla-like cephalic setæ number four, or possibly six, and are always small and very inconspicuous; they are situated somewhat behind the outer border of the truncate head. The lips, three in number, are sometimes single and sometimes double, and are supplied with papillæ, usually six, arranged around the mouth. The entrance to the pharynx is usually wide and is often striated longitudinally. The proportions of the pharynx vary much and serve very well to characterise the different species; sometimes the pharynx is shallow and cyathiform, and sometimes long and triquetrous. The variation in the armature of the pharynx is no less remarkable. Some species possess a single large dorsal tooth whose apex is directed forward and situated near the centre of the pharynx, while other species possess but a small or even rudimentary dorsal tooth; yet other species seem to entirely lack a dorsal tooth, and present instead a number of small teeth at the very base of the pharynx.

The œsophagus invariably possesses two well developed bulbs and sometimes three: of these the spheroidal median is the most conspicuous, being supplied with powerful radial muscles; the more elongated cardiac bulb is second in importance and is also supplied with well developed radial muscles; the pharyngeal bulb is the least conspicuous and is in fact nothing else than the expansion due to the presence of muscles attached to the parts of the pharynx. Of the intermediate tubular parts of the œsophagus, that between the pharynx and the median bulb is usually about half as wide as the conoid neck and twice as wide as the other,—that between the median and cardiac bulb,—and much less flexible. Some species possess a marked power of contracting and extending the neck; in the contracted state the intestine forms a shoulder in the cardiac region. Eye spots are unknown in the genus. The oblique nerve-ring encircles the œsophagus just behind the median bulb. The ventral excretory pore lies somewhat behind the nerve-ring. Lateral organs have been observed in but few of the species but this is doubtless due to insufficient care in observation; no doubt they exist in all the species. Where they have been observed they have been found to be placed opposite the pharynx and to be more or less elongated or elliptical in form and to have their long diameter placed longitudinally. In one species a glandular organ seems to exist in the œsophagus and to empty in the neighbourhood of the dorsal tooth. The intestine is usually thin-walled and ends in a rectum of the usual conoid form.

The female sexual organs are usually double, symmetrical and reflexed, but in two species are single and reflexed. The tail is invariably conoid and is usually exceedingly slender in its posterior part. Caudal glands of the usual form are absent, there being no terminal pore or spinneret. There are, however, on the tail of both sexes, commonly in front of its middle point, two lateral pores, one on either side, which are in my opinion the outlet of unicellular glands situated near the anus. These pores and glands exist also in the genus *Rhabditis.* Whether they are the morphological equivalents of the tail-glands in other genera I am not certain. It would seem that they cannot at any rate serve the same purpose as the ordinary arrangement as exhibited in *Plectus* and many other genera. The male has but one testicle, which is invariably reflexed near the extremity. The two arcuate spicula are equal in size and are elongated or linear and generally acute. Their proximal ends are usually cephalated by expansion ; accessory pieces parallel to the spicula are usually present. The peculiar papillæ found on the tail of the male are divided into three groups of three each, a grouping first made plain through the observations of Dr. Bütschli. The full complement of papillæ is not always present, or at least has not always been made out ; when however one or more pairs are absent, their position appears simply to stand vacant, and their absence does not much affect the position of those remaining. The first group may be described as the pre-anal group, and its members are ventrally submedian, or the posterior one may be lateral ; they are situated opposite to, or in the neighbourhood of, the spicula. The second group is post-anal and the members of it are often more widely separated than those of the pre-anal group, the anterior pair being usually ventrally submedian or even subdorsal. The posterior pair of the second group frequently lies farther back than the papillæ of the third group. The latter, also post-anal, are placed close together on the submedian line near where the tail diminishes most rapidly in size. In shape the papillæ resemble hairs, and, in fact, may be such, but with a special function. Those of the third group, however, are different, being often more like ordinary papillæ in structure. No other supplementary male organs are known in the genus except papillæ of another character near the anus.

There is an interesting dorsal organ on the head,—of unknown significance. It will be noticed in the description of the species in which it has been observed.

Key.

Pharynx with one or two large teeth.
    Tail end (female at least) encircled by a few conspicuous rings........................   1. *viviparus.*
    Tail end not so encircled.
        Length of the female not exceeding 1·mm.
            Body slender (little more than 2·6 %); neck long (23· %) ....   2. *parvus.*
            Body not so slender (3 % and over); neck shorter (13· % to 22· %).
                Female sexual organs asymmetrical (single).
                    Œsophagus 16 %.... ... .   3. *monhysteroides.*
                    Œsophagus 20 %...   4. *minor.*
                Female sexual organs double and symmetrical.
                    Reflexed ovaries crossing each other................. ....   5. *filicaudatus.*
                    Reflexed ovaries not crossing.
                        Œsophagus swollen just behind the pharynx................   6. *australis.*
                        Œsophagus not so swollen.
                            Body ·4 mm. long...   7. *minima.*
                            Body ·75 mm. long ....   8. *graminum.* *
        Length of the female 1·5 mm. or more.
            Throat or pharynx with two equally well developed teeth..................   9. *fluviatilis.*
             Throat or pharynx with only one well developed tooth.
                Tail about half as long as the worm.......... ....   10. *trichuris.*
                  Tail about one-third as long as the worm..................... ....   11. *striatus.*
                  Tail about one-seventh (15 %) as long as the worm.
                      Length 1·5 mm....... .. ..   12. *macrodon.*
                      Length 2· to 2·5 mm........... ....   13. *rivalis.*
Pharynx with only much less well developed teeth at the base.
    Female sexual organs single, asymmetrical............................ ....   14. *gracilis.*
    Female sexual organs double, symmetrical.
        Throat or pharynx shallow (half as deep as wide).
             Lips distinct; pharynx not striated..   15. *inermis.*
             Lips indistinct; pharynx striated...... ....   16. *similis.*
         Throat or pharynx as deep as wide, with small teeth at the base.
            Length exceeding 1·mm.
                Tail nearly one-third (30 %) as long as the worm......................   17. *longicauda.*
                Tail only one-fifth (16 to 20 %) as long as the worm.
                    Width 4·%....... ....   18. *filiformis.*
                    Width exceeding 7 %..   19. *albus.*

* The unknown female of *graminum* is assumed to have double and symmetrical sexual organs not crossing.

C

Key to the Males Described.

Pharynx with two large teeth.. 9. *fluviatilis.*
Pharynx with only one large tooth.
   Spicula unknown... 18. *filiformis.*
   Spicula not exceeding the anal body-diameter in length.
      Proximæ furcate.. .... 12. *macrodon.*
      Proximæ cephalated by constriction, not furcate.................................... 16. *similis.*
      Proximæ neither cephalated nor furcate... 8. *graminum.*
   Spicula exceeding the anal body-diameter in length.
      Tail 40 % or so.. 10. *trichuris.*
      Tail 30 % or so.
         Pharyngeal tooth basal.. 6. *australis.*
         Pharyngeal tooth not basal.
            Body longitudinally striated.. 11. *striatus.*
            Body not so striated.. 2. *parvus.*
      Tail about 15 % or 20 %.
         Length not exceeding 1 mm.
            Proximæ of the spicula geniculate.... .... 17. *longicauda.*
            Proximæ of the spicula not geniculate.
               Throat or pharynx with a well developed tooth.................. 7. *minima.*
               Throat or pharynx with no well developed tooth................. 14. *gracilis.*
         Length 2·5 mm. .... 13. *rivalis.*

1. **D. viviparus,** von Linstow. $\frac{1\cdot6}{1\cdot6} \frac{7}{7} \frac{14\cdot}{8\cdot1} \frac{50\cdot}{8\cdot1} \frac{86\cdot}{1\cdot3}$ 1·8 mm. Cuticle finely transversely striated. In front of the anus three, and on the anterior third of the tail five, prominent rings encircle the body. On the ventral side of the hindermost of these rings occurs a circular organ with a circular centre, the whole being as wide as the tail at that point. Head truncate, but with a broad projection at the mouth ; setæ none ; lips uncertain ; pharynx as deep as the head is wide and two-thirds as wide as the head, constricted in the middle, with some teeth of unequal size at the base ; pharyngeal swelling elongated, tapering behind ; median bulb considerably behind the middle of the neck ; posterior swelling much elongated, tapering anteriorly ; tail conical, tapering from in front of the anus ; caudal glands none ; viviparous ; embryos slender, without the chitinous structure on the head.

Hab.—Water plants, Germany. It is perhaps questionable whether this is a *Diplogaster.*

2. **D. parvus,** n.sp. Female unknown. $\frac{1\cdot6}{1\cdot3} \frac{15\cdot}{2\cdot4} \frac{23\cdot}{8\cdot6} \frac{^{\cdot}M^{30}}{2\cdot6} \frac{68\cdot}{2\cdot3}$ 4 mm. Neck conoid ; head truncate, with six lips, each with one papilla ; pharynx elongated, crooked, anterior part wider, the tooth appearing as a prominence and without a distinct and projecting apex ; œsophagus slender, the anterior part being only one-third as wide as the neck ; bulbs one-half as wide as the neck ; intestine three-fourths as wide as the body ;

position of the excretory pore unknown; two wings on the lateral field separated by a distance equal to one-fourth the width of the body. The tail is conical, and is arcuate in the anterior part. The anus is rather prominent. The two equal elongated-cuneiform acute arcuate spicula slide in an accessory piece having a backward-pointing somewhat hook-shaped process, which if straightened out and extended forward would reach nearly to the proximæ. The male papillæ are finger-shaped and are arranged as follows: 1, a sublateral pair as far in front of the proximal ends of the spicula as the latter are in front of the anus; 2, one submedian pair just in front of the proximæ; 3, one subventral pair just in front of the anus; 4, one submedian pair as far behind the anus as the first pair mentioned above is in front of it; 5, and finally, a ventral post-anal group (two pairs?) twice as far from the anus as those last mentioned. All these details, as well as many others, are set forth on Pl. IV.

Hab.—On decaying outside sheaths of young banana plants, Fiji, July, 1891.

3. **D. monhysteroides,** Bütschli. $\frac{1 \; 7 \; 17 \cdot \; 50 \cdot \; 58 \cdot}{1 \; 1 \; 1 \; 38 \; 7}$ ·78 mm. The neck diminishes more rapidly than in *filicaudatus;* it resembles that species, however, in the structure of the pharynx, except that the pharynx of *monhysteroides* is somewhat narrower. The female sexual organs are asymmetrical, there being, however, a posterior sterile branch reaching nearly to the anus.

Hab.—This species, which much resembles the *filicaudatus* of the same author, was found with that species in cow-dung, Germany.

4. **D. minor,** n.sp. $\frac{1\cdot6 \; 13 \cdot \; 20 \cdot \; \cdot49^{20} \; 68 \cdot}{17 \; 29 \; 29 \; 32 \; 2}$ ·5 mm. No markings were observed on the cuticle, which was without hairs as well. A three-lipped truncate head surmounts the conoid neck. Each lip bears a setose papilla. The pharynx is about as deep as the head is wide, and in its widest part is half as wide as the head; the single large acute dorsal tooth springs from the base of the pharynx and extends nearly half-way to the mouth. The œsophagus does not expand to receive the pharynx but assumes immediately a width three-fifths as great as the neck and so continues to the ellipsoidal median bulb, which is three-fourths as wide as the neck; behind the median bulb the œsophagus is narrower, passing through the nerve-ring with a width one-third as great as that of the neck but expanding finally to form a bulb somewhat smaller than the median bulb. The intestine, which is separated from the œsophagus by a distinct cardiac constriction, is rather coarsely granular, and ends in a rectum having a length equal to that of the anal body-diameter. The conical tail is excessively fine near its end. No caudal glands were seen. The reflexed part of the ovary extends nearly half-way back to the inconspicuous vulva. The rather thick-shelled eggs are a little more than twice as long as the body is wide, and one-third to one-fourth as wide as long, being, therefore, of such a large size that the uterus will

contain but one at a time. I do not know whether segmentation begins before the eggs are deposited. Male unknown. Figures of this species are given on Pl. IV. along with those of *D. parvus.*

Hab.—On decaying outside sheaths of young banana plants, Fiji, July, 1891.

5. D. filicaudatus, Bütschli. $\frac{2 \cdot (7) \quad 1 \quad 13 \cdot \quad 60' \quad 68 \cdot}{2 \cdot (7) \quad 1 \quad 1 \quad 8 \quad 1} 1 \cdot mm.$ Neck conoid; cephalic setæ apparently four; pharynx nearly as deep as the head is wide, and more than one-half as wide as the head; dorsal tooth projecting and thumb-shaped, reaching nearly to the middle of the pharynx; near the bottom of the pharynx two small submedian teeth. The uterus appears never to contain more than one egg at a time.

Hab.—Cow-dung, Germany.

6. D. australis, n.sp. $\frac{1 \cdot 4 \quad 12 \cdot \quad 17 \cdot 5 \quad 49' \quad 77 \cdot}{2 \cdot \quad 27 \quad 8 \cdot \quad 3 \cdot 3 \quad 2} \cdot 59 mm.$ I cannot state positively whether this female is not the mate of that described later on under the name *D. graminum.* They were found together and have the same proportions, but there are marked differences in the structure of the pharynx in the two specimens. In the present species the cuticle is finely transversely striated. The pharynx is twice as deep as wide, being simply deeply cyathiform in shape, and two-fifths as wide as the head. The dorsal tooth is simple in character and extends half-way to the lips. Just behind the pharynx the œsophagus is somewhat swollen, its greatest width in this part being considerably less than that of the ellipsoidal median bulb, which is four-fifths as wide as the middle of the neck. The posterior bulb is longer and narrower than the median. Between the pharyngeal and the median bulbs the œsophagus is two-fifths as wide as the neck, but between the median and cardiac bulbs it is only one-third as wide as the neck. The intestine is very narrow at first,—only one-fourth as wide as the body,—but soon becomes three-fourths as wide as the body. The narrow rectum considerably exceeds the anal body-diameter in length. The reflexed ovaries reach nearly back to the vulva and contain numerous ova arranged in several rows. The eggs are twice as long as the body is wide and one-third as wide as long. The tail is conoid, being setaceous in the posterior half.

Hab.—Grass, Sydney, New South Wales, Australia.

7. D. minima, n.sp. $\frac{2 \cdot \quad 17 \cdot \quad 22 \cdot \quad 43 \cdot^{28} \quad 68 \cdot}{2 \cdot \quad 44 \quad 46 \quad 46 \quad 24} \cdot 4 mm.$ The cuticle is traversed longitudinally by about fourteen equidistant striæ or wings, so arranged that one of them does *not* fall on a lateral line, resolvable into dots ·7µ apart, thus indicating ·the presence also of about six hundred transverse striæ. Neither setæ nor lateral organs were seen. The triquetrous pharynx is about one-fifth as wide as the head; the dorsal tooth is elongated and projects but slightly, although its apex approaches to near the lips. The ellipsoidal median bulb is two-thirds as wide as the neck, the cardiac bulb being, as usual, somewhat smaller and weaker. The transparent thick-walled

intestine is two-thirds as wide as the body, its cells containing coarse granules. The cardia is deep and the cardiac cavity is distinct. The anterior half of the tail is conoid, the posterior half setaceous. The reflexed ovaries reach nearly to the slightly projecting vulva. The thin-shelled eggs are two-thirds as long as the body is wide and two-thirds as wide as long, and begin segmenting while in the uterus. $\frac{1·7}{?}\frac{17·}{4·6}\frac{23·}{4·6}\frac{·M^{40}}{4·6}\frac{78·}{3·6}$ ·36 mm. The anterior two-fifths of the male tail is conoid and ventrally arcuate; thence it is setaceous. The anal region is slightly elevated. Of the male papillæ at least all three pairs of the closely approximated third group and four other pairs are present. Of these latter four, three pairs occur opposite the middle of the spicula, two being ventrally submedian and close together, and one lateral, slightly farther back; the fourth pair—lateral—is as far behind the anus as the foremost of the other three is in front of it. The closely approximated three pairs, situated where the tail suddenly narrows, are associated with a slight ventral swelling. The spicula are linear, gently arcuate and nearly twice as long as the anal body-diameter. The slender accessory pieces are somewhat sigmoid in form, their internal ends turning forward, while their opposite ends are applied to the distal parts of the spicula. Only a small portion of the testicle is reflexed. The testicle and vas deferens are of about equal length.

Hab.—Decaying outside sheaths of banana plants, Fiji, July, 1891.

8.. **D. graminum**, n.sp. Female unknown.* $\frac{1·5}{1·9}\frac{9·6}{2·6}\frac{15·6}{2·9}\frac{·M^{35}}{3·2}\frac{69·}{2·6}$ ·63 mm. The cuticle is marked transversely by very fine striæ. The pharynx is as deep as the head is wide, and, when seen in profile, appears much narrower in its posterior half than in its anterior half because of the presence in the posterior part of the large and pointed dorsal tooth; anteriorly the pharynx is half as wide as the head. The ellipsoidal median bulb is two-thirds as wide as the neck and is less elongated and more pronounced than the posterior bulb. The tubular part of the œsophagus is rather uniform in diameter, the anterior half being but little wider than the posterior half. The ventral excretory pore is situated somewhat nearer the cardiac than the median bulb. The granular intestine is three-fourths as wide as the body. The anterior fifth of the tail is ventrally arcuate and conoid; thence onward it is setaceous. The arcuate-cunciform spicula are equal to the anal body-diameter in length and are supplied with arcuate accessory pieces half as long. These latter are slender and make a slight angle with the spicula. Six pairs of papillæ were seen : 1, a ventrally submedian pre-anal pair opposite the proximal ends of the spicula ; 2, a ventrally submedian pair somewhat behind the anus ; 3, three approximated submedian pairs somewhat in front of the place where the tail becomes rather suddenly setaceous ; 4, a dorsal pair (or only one, I am not positive) somewhat behind the three pairs just mentioned.

Hab.—Grass, Sydney, New South Wales, Australia.

* See, however, *D. australis*, p. 269.

9. **D. fluviatilis**, de Man. $\frac{1\ 7}{1\ 7}\frac{14\cdot}{?}\frac{\cdot 50\cdot}{2\cdot 1}\frac{89\cdot}{?}$ 1·8 mm. Cuticle very finely transversely striated; neck conoid, diminishing much; cephalic setæ two, lateral; lateral organs small clefts, alike in both sexes; pharynx with two large teeth of equal size, both edged and pointed and crossed when at rest, in the living state continually biting together; wall of the pharynx in front of the teeth longitudinally striated; portion of the œsophageal tube behind the stout median bulb two-thirds as long as the remainder; tail conical to the hair-fine terminus; oviparous. $\frac{?\ ?}{?\ ?}\frac{14}{17}\frac{M}{?}\frac{89\cdot}{?}$ 1·8 mm. With the exception of two small pairs near the middle of the tail, all the male papillæ are bristle-shaped. The bristle-shaped papillæ are arranged as follows : one pair submedian just in front of the anus, one pair lateral just in front of the anus; one pair submedian a little behind the anus, one pair submedian near the middle of the tail, one lateral pair between the two pairs last mentioned, and, finally, one lateral pair far back. Spicula stout, plump, arcuate; accessory pieces long, rod-shaped.

Hab.—Found in water, Holland ; less common than *D. rivalis.*

10. **D. trichuris**, n.sp. $\frac{2}{2}\frac{8\cdot7}{2\cdot6}\frac{12\cdot}{2\cdot6}\frac{\cdot 28\cdot}{3\cdot1}^{16}\frac{40\cdot}{1\cdot8}$ 1·6 mm. The cuticle is traversed longitudinally by about forty wings and transversely by numerous striæ. The convex-conoid head bears four very short and inconspicuous spreading submedian cephalic setæ arranged opposite the apex of the conspicuous dorsal tooth. Six labial papillæ surround the mouth-opening, which is longitudinally striated inside and supported by longitudinal ribs. The elongated-elliptical lateral organs, one-eighth as wide as the head, are situated parallel to and opposite the middle of the pharynx. This latter is narrow, being only one-fourth as wide as deep, and contains a single large hamate dorsal tooth whose apex is nearly on a level with the lips. This tooth is so large as to pretty well close up the mouth opening. All the organs in the neck are quite typical. The ellipsoidal median and cardiac bulbs are of nearly equal size : though the cardiac if anything is the larger, the median is manifestly the more perfectly developed; they are two-thirds to three-fourths as wide as the neck. The portion of the œsophagus between the

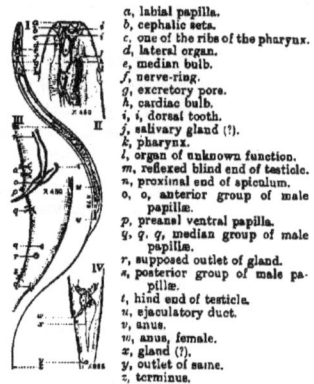

a, labial papilla.
b, cephalic seta.
c, one of the ribs of the pharynx.
d, lateral organ.
e, median bulb.
f, nerve-ring.
g, excretory pore.
h, cardiac bulb.
i, i, dorsal tooth.
j, salivary gland (?).
k, pharynx.
l, organ of unknown function.
m, reflexed blind end of testicle.
n, proximal end of spiculum.
o, o, anterior group of male papillæ.
p, preanal ventral papilla.
q, q, q, median group of male papillæ.
r, supposed outlet of gland.
s, posterior group of male papillæ.
t, hind end of testicle.
u, ejaculatory duct.
v, anus.
w, anus, female.
x, gland (?).
y, outlet of same.
z, terminus.

Fig. 3.—I, male *Diplogaster trichuris ;* II and III, head and anal region of the same, more highly magnified ; IV, anal region of the female of the same worm.

pharynx and the median bulb is one-half as wide as the neck and about twice as wide as that part between the two bulbs. The intestine is two-thirds as wide as the body. The conoid rectum is one and one-half times as long as the anal body-diameter. The reflexed ovaries extend back nearly to the inconspicuous vulva. The position of the ventral gland remains unknown, but the ventral pore, its outlet is situated just behind the nerve-ring. Two lateral glandular organs occur opposite the rectum, each emptying through a lateral pore near the middle of the thicker conoid anterior part of the tail. Inside the œsophagus, too, a gland appears to exist and to empty its secretion into the pharynx in the neighbourhood of the dorsal tooth. A dorsal organ occurs on the head, at least of the male; this I have figured. Its function is a mystery to me; I can only suggest that it is a special male organ of some sort, my reasons being briefly these :—1. I observed it only on the males; nevertheless as I have seen but few females it may have been present on their heads and have escaped me. 2. Oerley has described a "lateral organ" as existing only on the male of his *macrodon*. Is this not perhaps the same organ that I have observed? I think it more than probable. These reasons are not a sufficient basis for a pronounced opinion, but they will serve to call particular attention to this organ in future. The male formula is as follows. $\frac{1\cdot8}{1\cdot7}\ \frac{9\cdot}{2\cdot5}\ \frac{13\cdot6}{2\cdot5}\ \frac{\cdot M^{38}}{2\cdot5}\ \frac{67\cdot}{1\cdot8}$ 1·27 mm. The tail is similar in form to that of the female. Beside the full complement of nine pairs of finger-shaped papillæ there is a pair of low ventral papillæ just in front of the anus. The nine pairs are arranged as follows : 1, two closely approximated submedian pairs opposite the middle of the distal half of the spicula ; 2, a sublateral pair a little farther forward than the low ventral pre-anal pair mentioned above ; 3, a submedian pair just in front of the pores forming the outlet of the lateral caudal glands, or in other words just behind the middle of the conoid part of the tail ; 4, three closely approximated subventral pairs just in front of where the tail diminishes rather suddenly and becomes setaceous, or in other words near the end of the conoid part of the tail ; 5, a subdorsal pair somewhat behind the three pairs just described. The linear spicula taper gradually, but not uniformly, to a slender point; the proximal parts are narrowed also. The accessory pieces are half as long as the spicula and are arranged parallel to them. Only a small portion of the testicle near the blind end is reflexed. The testicle has about the same length as the neck of the worm and occupies a position half way between the cardiac region and the anus. The vas deferens is of somewhat smaller diameter than the testicle and is connected with it by a narrow passage. The ejaculatory duct is apparently quite short.

Hab.—Grass, Sydney, New South Wales, Australia.

11. **D. striatus**, Bütschli. $\frac{?}{?}\ \frac{?}{?}\ \frac{13\cdot3}{?}\ \frac{\cdot50\cdot}{?}\ \frac{71\cdot}{?}$ 1·8 mm. The cuticle is traversed longitudinally by about forty striæ; head rounded-truncate near the mouth, with apparently four setæ; lips scarcely to be detected; pharynx two-thirds as deep as the head is wide, longitudinally striated anteriorly, containing two very small submedian teeth at

the base, and one well-developed and projecting dorsal tooth extending three-fourths the distance to the lips; according to Bütschli, excretory ducts on both sides of the body; uteri containing but few eggs; oviparous; male tail convex-conoid for a distance equal to twice the anal body-diameter, being at that point as wide as the spicula and continuing conoid to the exceedingly fine terminus; two pairs of pre-anal papillæ, one opposite the proximæ and the second opposite the middle of the spicula, both submedian; post-anal papillæ, two pairs submedian opposite the anus, two pairs submedian near the middle of the large part of the tail, and the remaining four pairs approximated near the commencement of the narrow part of the tail; spicula linear, one and one-half times as long as the anal body-diameter, distal halves only arcuate to the acute points; accessory pieces less than half as long as the spicula.

Hab.—Found among decaying masses on the surface of the river Main at Frankfort, Germany.

12. **D. macrodon**, Oerley. $\frac{9\ 7\ 12\cdot1\ \cdot44''\ 83'}{13\ 7\ 18\ \ 22\ 16}$ 1·6 mm. Cuticle with about one thousand transverse striæ; neck nearly cylindrical, convex-conoid near the head; head rounded in front; no cephalic setæ; lips prominent; lateral organs said to be circular with a spot in the middle, nearly as wide as the pharynx, behind the base of which they are situated; pharynx irregularly cylindrical, one-third as wide as the head; dorsal tooth reaching half-way to the lips, the other two only one-third as long but equally pointed; median bulb central, prolate, two-thirds as wide as the neck, somewhat wider than the conoid posterior swelling; the intestine is half as wide as the body and is marked off from the œsophagus by a deep and narrow constriction; excretory pore at 10%, that is, somewhat in front of the cardiac constriction; tail conical from the inconspicuous anus; terminus wider than usual, *i.e.*, not hair-fine; vulva depressed; eggs ellipsoidal, as long as the body is wide and half as wide as long; viviparous; reflexed portions of the ovaries reaching one-fourth the way back to the vulva. $\frac{1\cdot\ 7\ 12\cdot\ \cdot M^{64}\ 87\cdot}{13\ 7\ 25\ \ 25\ 9}$ 1·mm. Male tail conical, its terminus hair-fine; papillæ as follows : one pre-anal pair, submedian, opposite the proximæ; one post-anal ventral near the anus; the remainder post-anal, of which the first is as far behind the anus as the pre-anal submedian pair is in front of it, the second considerably behind the middle of the tail, and the third half-way between the second pair and the terminus; spicula elongated, two-thirds as long as the anal body-diameter, their proximæ enlarged and apparently furcate.

Hab.—Found in Hungary.

13. **D. rivalis**, Leydig. $\frac{1\cdot\ 8\cdot\ 11\cdot8\ \cdot45''\ 86\cdot}{13\ 15\ 16\ \ 9\ 7}$ 2·5 mm. The skin is marked by about thirteen hundred transverse striæ. The truncate head is almost imperceptibly expanded. Six long and fine cephalic setæ surround the mouth, and in addition the male is said to possess a second row of subcephalic setæ. The projecting oval lateral

organs are situated opposite the anterior part of the pharynx and are possessed of a horny centre, being smaller in the females and more like clefts.   The stoutly built pharynx is supplied at the middle with an encircling ring ; in front of this ring it is longitudinally striated.   The dorsal tooth reaches beyond the ring, and there are one or two others near the base of the pharynx.   The median bulb is two-thirds as wide as the neck, while the cardiac bulb is an elongated swelling, not bulbous.   The brown and somewhat tessellated intestine is marked off from the œsophagus by a distinct constriction ; it is said to be composed of not above three rows of cells.   The rectum is three-fourths as long as the anal body-diameter.   The ventral excretory pore occurs at 9%, that is, considerably in front of the cardiac constriction.   The finely-pointed conoid tail is slightly concave somewhat behind the middle and bears a pair of lateral papillæ (pores ?).   This species is viviparous, the uteri sometimes containing a dozen embryos.   The reflexed ovaries sometimes meet and cross.   The proportions of the male are precisely those of his mate, but he is somewhat smaller, usually measuring only 2·mm.   Papillæ as follows : only one pre-anal submedian pair just in front of the anus ; three lateral equidistant pairs on the anterior half of the tail beginning near the anus ; two pairs submedian opposite the lateral three pairs ; two pairs subventral close together opposite the anterior pairs of the preceding two groups.   The pores (?) found on the female occur also on the male.   Spicula slender, arcuate, one and one-half times as long as the anal body-diameter.   Accessory pieces one-half as long as the spicula, slipper-shaped, plump, and nearly surrounding the tips of the spicula.   Synonym, *D. fictor,* Bastian.

Hab.—Found among fresh-water algæ in Western Europe and England.   Has the habit of becoming suddenly still, as if dead.

14. **D. gracilis,** Bütschli. $\frac{1\cdot6}{5\cdot}\frac{?}{5\cdot6}\frac{19\cdot}{8\cdot}\frac{'66\cdot^{38}}{8\cdot1\cdot4\cdot}\frac{70\cdot}{}$ ♀mm. Neck convex-conoid ; body wider in the middle than at the vulva, namely 7·3 °/$_o$; head rounded-truncate ; cephalic setæ six ; lips six, broad and flat ; pharynx cylindroid, composed of several horny pieces, with possibly two rudimentary teeth at base ; both bulbs elongated, the median central, the cardiac weaker ; œsophagus twice, the bulbs three times, as wide as the pharynx ; intestine large, thin-walled, forming a shoulder in the cardiac region, separated from the œsophagus by a deep constriction so that the collum is only one-fifth as wide ; cardia broad and distinct ; cardiac cavity two-thirds as wide as the body and very long ; rectum half as long as the anal body-diameter ; tail concave-conoid, diminishing in the anterior fifth to a width as great as the head, and thence conical to the hair-fine terminus ; vulva inconspicuous, with almost invisible radial muscles ; vagina one-third as long as the body is wide ; eggs same size as median bulb ; ovary reaching at least three-fourths the way back to the vulva.   The proportions of the male agree fairly with those of the female, but the tail is shorter.   Papillæ

D

as follows : lateral, two pairs opposite the spicula, one opposite the anterior part, the other opposite the posterior part ; two pairs submedian close together opposite the anus ; three pairs, two submedian and one lateral, just behind the middle of the wide portion of the tail ; one pair lateral near the end of the wide part of the tail ; spicula very slender, one and one-half times as long as the anal body-diameter ; accessory pieces none (?).

Hab.—Found in dung, Germany.

15. **D. inermis**, Bütschli. $\frac{1\cdot4\quad 19\cdot\quad 29\cdot\quad ?\quad 77\cdot5}{4\cdot7\quad 7\cdot6\quad 9\cdot\quad ?\quad ?}$ ·5 mm. Female only known. Neck conoid; head truncate ; cephalic setæ six, very short; lips six, large, broad and flat; pharynx one-half as wide as the head, cylindroid, one-half as deep as wide, with three teeth at base not well developed ; the three bulbs of equal diameter and the median bulb central ; intestine at once twice as wide as the bulbs, separated from the œsophagus by a distinct constriction.

Hab.—Found on roots of garlic which had been attacked by insect larvæ, Germany.

16. **D. similis**, Bütschli. $\frac{?\quad ?\quad 9\cdot\quad ?\quad 71\cdot}{?\quad ?\quad ?\quad ?\quad ?}$ 1·2 mm. Head rounded-truncate ; cephalic setæ six, broad and extremely short ; lips indistinct ; pharynx longitudinally striated, half as wide as the head, half as deep as wide, with three teeth at the base, the dorsal one somewhat larger; eggs ·05 mm. long. A young male gave the following dimensions : $\frac{?\quad ?\quad 15\cdot\quad \text{M}\quad 67\cdot}{?\quad ?\quad ?\quad 3\cdot9\quad ?}$ ·6 mm. Tail contracting but little at first, but behind its middle point becoming conoid suddenly, narrows to a breadth not greater than that of the spicula, and continues thence narrow and conical to the hair-fine terminus ; pre-anal setiform papillæ as follows : one pair submedian just in front of the spicula ; one pair submedian opposite the middle of the spicula. Post-anal papillæ as follows : two pairs dorsal submedian, one near middle of wide anterior part of the tail (these are perhaps the pores), the other where the tail narrows suddenly ; three lateral pairs closely approximated just in front of the pair last mentioned ; one ventrally submedian setiform pair somewhat behind the anus ; one subventral pair close to anus, not setiform ; spicula one-sixth as broad as long, rather blunt, nearly straight, equalling the anal body-diameter in length ; accessory pieces two-thirds as long as the spicula.

Hab.—Unknown to me.

17. **D. longicauda**, Claus. $\frac{2\cdot\ (?)\quad ?\quad 15\cdot4\quad \cdot50\prime\quad 71\cdot}{3\cdot8\ (?)\quad ?\quad ?\quad 5\cdot5\quad ?}$ 1·1 mm. Cuticle transversely striated ; head truncate ; cephalic setæ six, very short ; lips six, distinct, rounded ; pharynx cylindroid, half as long as the head is wide, and as deep as wide, its walls divided into anterior and posterior parts composed of distinct pieces ; teeth three, at the base of the pharynx, constantly clapping together ; lateral fields broad ; eggs ·054 mm. long. $\frac{2\cdot\ (?)\quad ?\quad 15\cdot4\quad \text{M}\quad 88\cdot}{3\cdot8\ (?)\quad ?\quad ?\quad 5\cdot5\quad 3\cdot0}$ 1·mm. Male tail convex-conoid to in front of the middle, where it is

twice as wide as the spicula, thence conical to the hair-fine terminus ; papillæ as follows, all (?) setose : one submedian setose pair in front of the spicula ; three lateral pairs, one opposite the anus, one where the tail suddenly diminishes in size, and one half-way between ; two ventral submedian rather close together somewhat behind the anus ; and three closely approximated subventral pairs at the end of the large part of the tail ; spicula linear, one and one-half times as long as the anal body-diameter, posterior two-thirds arcuate, proximal ends geniculate ; accessory pieces one-fourth as long as the spicula, and seeming to pretty nearly surround them.

Hab.—Decaying fungi, Frankfort, Germany.

18. **D. filiformis**, Bastian. $\frac{1\cdot6}{2\cdot6}\frac{?}{1}\frac{17\cdot}{4\cdot}\frac{50\cdot}{4\cdot1}\frac{62\cdot}{2\cdot6}$ ·62mm. Cuticula marked by about five hundred transverse striæ, also (?) with longitudinal striæ ; head truncate ; pharynx prismoid, half as wide as the head, deeper than wide, with three teeth at the base ; bulbs elongated, half as wide as the neck, the median central; cardiac collum distinct; intestine as wide as the bulbs ; rectum two-thirds as long as the anal body-diameter ; tail conical to just behind the middle, thence hair-fine. $\frac{1\cdot8}{2\cdot6}\frac{?}{?}\frac{17\cdot}{3\cdot5}\frac{M}{3\cdot5}\frac{76\cdot}{3\cdot1}$ ·58mm. Tail like that of the female ; spicula could not be detected.

Hab.—England.

19. **D. albus**, Bastian. $\frac{2\cdot}{4\cdot}\frac{?}{?}\frac{18\cdot}{6\cdot5}\frac{50\cdot}{7\cdot6}\frac{84\cdot}{4\cdot}$ ·60mm. Cuticle finely transversely striated ; neck conoid ; head truncate ; lips probably six, but very indistinct ; pharynx half as wide as the head, as deep as wide, with three teeth at the base ; median bulb central, elongated, half as wide as the head ; cardiac bulb spherical, two-thirds as wide as the median bulb and connected with it by a constriction one-fourth as wide as the adjacent part of the neck, that is, only half as wide as the anterior part of the œsophagus ; cardiac collum distinct ; intestine at once half as wide as the body ; rectum as long as the anal body-diameter ; tail conical to the pointed terminus. Male unknown.

Hab.—England.

20. **D. micans**, Max Schultze. Insufficiently known.

21. **D. liratus**, Schneider *(Leptodera lirata).* Insufficiently known.

Genus RHABDITIS.

1. **R. filiformis**, Bütschli. (?). I am not certain that this little species, of which I have seen only the female, is in reality that described by Bütschli under the name *filiformis.* The specimens seen by me gave dimensions as follows: $\frac{3\cdot6}{2\cdot6}\frac{1}{?}\frac{20\cdot}{4\cdot}\frac{\cdot42^{33}}{4\cdot}\frac{09\cdot}{2\cdot}$ ·54mm. Cuticle plainly but finely transversely striated ; neck nearly cylindrical to behind the

pharynx, then convex-conoid to the mouth, which is one-fourth as wide as the base of the neck; lip-region half as wide as the prolate cardiac bulb; only traces of lips; no setæ or papillæ on the head; œsophagus in the anterior half fusiform and about half as wide as the neck, thence narrowing gradually to a tube one-fifth as wide as the neck; cardiac sucking bulb one-half as wide as the neck; cardiac collum distinct, the constriction deep; intestine thick-walled, four-fifths as wide as the body, with a thick transparent lining; cardia small, the cavity large; rectum narrow, nearly twice as long as the anal body-diameter, separated from the intestine by a distinct constriction; ventral excretory pore somewhat behind the middle of the neck (12·5 %); wings of the cuticle nearly as far apart as the opposite sides of the pharynx; tail conoid from the distinct anus, its terminus hair-fine; near the anus two lateral glands which empty through lateral pores at the beginning of the second sixth of the tail; vulva depressed; vagina very short; reflexed ovaries reaching half-way back to the vulva; eggs as long as the body is wide and two-thirds as wide as long. Sketches of this little species are given on Pl. 1.

Hab.—Grass after rain, Sydney, New South Wales, Australia.

2. R. pellioides, Bütschli. $\frac{1\cdot0\quad 13\cdot\quad 19\cdot\quad \cdot49'^{42}\quad 8^{8\cdot}}{1\cdot8\quad 3\cdot8\quad 4\cdot3\quad 4\cdot7\quad 2\cdot5}$ ·8 to 1· mm. Cuticle transversely striated; neck conoid, tapering more rapidly near the head; head truncate; lips six, hemispherical, each with a papilla; pharynx simple, prismoid, one-third as wide as the head; median and cardiac bulbs powerful, subspherical, two-thirds as wide as the neck, the median situated in the middle of the neck; œsophageal tube in front of the median bulb half as wide as the neck, behind the bulb one-third; ventral excretory pore somewhat nearer the cardiac than the median bulb; intestine rather thick-walled, three-fourths as wide as the body; rectum considerably longer than the anal body-diameter; tail concave-conoid; vulva inconspicuous; reflexed portions of the ovaries reaching half-way back to the vulva; eggs nearly as long as the body is wide and two-thirds as wide as long; viviparous or ovoviviparous; lateral pores near the middle of the tail. $\frac{3\cdot7\quad 17\cdot\quad 27\cdot\quad \cdot7^{57}\quad 94\cdot}{3\cdot2\quad 4\cdot0\quad 5\cdot3\quad 3\cdot4\quad 3\cdot}$ ·5 mm. Male tail conical, completely enveloped in the bursa, which springs from opposite the middle of the spicula; ribs of the bursa nine, in three similar rather indistinct groups because the spaces between the groups are not much greater than that between the individual ribs of a given group; anterior group just in front of the anus, posterior group near the end of the tail; spicula linear, tapering gradually from near the proximæ to an acute point, more than twice as long as the tail; proximæ cephalated by constriction. Detailed drawings are given on Pl. iii.

Hab.—Cosmopolitan; Europe, Australia, Fiji. I think there can be no doubt that this worm recorded now from Australia and Fiji is identical with Bütschli's species. I have found it on fresh grass and on dead sheaths of banana plants.

3. **R. australis**, n.sp. (?). $\frac{1 \cdot \;\; 12 \cdot \;\; 17 \cdot \;\; \cdot 55 \cdot^{50} \;\; 93 \cdot 2}{1 \cdot 5 \;\; 3 \cdot 8 \;\; 4 \cdot 3 \;\; 4 \cdot 6 \;\; 2 \cdot 4}$ 1·1 mm.   Cuticula finely transversely striated; neck conoid, convex anteriorly; head somewhat pointed, truncate at the lips; lips six, conical, each with a setose papilla; pharynx simple, prismoid, tapering at the base, about one-third as wide as the head and more than twice as deep as wide; anterior three-fifths of the œsophagus cylindroid, about one-third as wide as the corresponding part of the neck; cardiac sucking bulb ellipsoidal, half as wide as the base of the neck, connected with the wider anterior three-fifths of the œsophagus by a tube one-fifth as wide as the corresponding part of the neck; intestine thin-walled, four-fifths as wide as the body; rectum as long as the anal body-diameter; ventral excretory pore just behind the nerve-ring; tail conical; vulva slightly elevated; vagina extending forward half-way to the cardiac region and containing spermatozoa near the flexure; ovary very long, reflexed and extending backward to near the anus; eggs ellipsoidal, as long as the body is wide and two-thirds as wide as long, thin-shelled, perhaps deposited before segmentation begins.

Hab.—Grass, Sydney, New South Wales, Australia.

4. **R. monhystera**, Bütschli. $\frac{2 \cdot 4 \;\; 12 \cdot \;\; 20 \cdot \;\; \cdot 80 \cdot^{40} \;\; 90 \cdot}{2 \cdot 4 \;\; 4 \cdot 7 \;\; 5 \cdot 4 \;\; 5 \cdot \;\; 2 \cdot 4}$ ·7 mm. The cuticula of this cosmopolitan species is traversed by about four hundred transverse striæ. The posterior half of the neck is conoid, the anterior half convex-conoid. The truncate head, devoid of setæ, is surmounted by six spherical lips having a height equal to one-third the length of the pharynx, and each surmounted by a conspicuous projecting papilla. The simple cylindroid pharynx is about one-fourth as wide as long. The median œsophageal bulb is of about the same length as the pharynx and is one-half as wide as the neck; that portion of the œsophagus leading to it is a little more than one-third as wide as the neck, and that portion leading from it to the posterior bulb is a trifle narrower than that. The prolate posterior bulb is a little wider still than the median bulb and contains a distinct chitinous valvular apparatus. The cardiac collum is distinct. The ventral excretory pore is situated opposite the anterior part of the hindmost bulb. The oblique nerve-ring passes ventrally backward. The tail is conical to the pointed terminus. The lateral fields are one-fourth as wide as the body. The narrow, reflexed ovary extends from one-fourth to one-half the distance back to the vulva. Passing round the bend the ova are fertilised and then develop in the uterus, those near the vulva being always more advanced than the others. $\frac{2 \cdot 6 \;\; 15 \cdot 7 \;\; 22 \cdot 4 \;\; \cdot M^{60} \;\; 97 \cdot}{3 \cdot 0 \;\; 6 \cdot 1 \;\; 6 \cdot 8 \;\; 7 \cdot 7 \;\; 3 \cdot}$ ·9 mm. The tail of the male is conical and pointed; it is completely enveloped by the bursa, which begins opposite the proximal ends of the spicula. The ribs of the bursa are distributed in three groups: 1, a pre-anal group of two opposite the middle of the spicula; 2, a post-anal group of three occupying the anterior third of that part of the bursa behind the anus; 3, a post-anal group of three near the end of the tail. I saw on one specimen what appeared to be a ventral

papilla near the middle of the tail. The straight equal linear acute spicula are one and one-half times longer than the tail and are barely cephalated by expansion. The accessory piece is parallel to the spicula and is one-half as long as they. The reflexed portion of the testicle reaches one-fourth the distance back to the anus. The reader will do well to consult the drawings on Pl. III.

Hab.—Decaying leaves of banana plants, Fiji, July, 1891. These worms are common on fresh and living grass, and on celery in Australia.

5. **R. coronata**, n.sp. $\frac{6 \cdot \quad 17 \cdot \quad 26 \cdot \quad \cdot 55^{\cdot 30} \quad 81 \cdot}{1 \cdot \quad 4\frac{1}{2} \quad 5\frac{1}{2} \quad 5\frac{1}{2} \quad 2\frac{1}{2}}$ ·36 mm. is the formula for the only specimen seen. The cuticula was striated. The head was surmounted by six (?) conical lips each turned outwards. The cylindroid pharynx was about one-tenth as wide as long. The ellipsoidal median bulb was one-half as wide as the middle of the neck, and was situated half way between the mouth and the beginning of the intestine. The posterior bulb was of the same shape as the median, but was about half as wide again. Those portions of the œsophagus lying between the pharynx and the median bulb and between the median and posterior bulbs were equal in length but unequal in width, the latter being of the same width as the pharynx, while the former was twice as wide. The cardiac collum was distinct. The intestine was three-fourths as wide as the body. The ventral excretory pore was situated a little behind the nerve-ring. The latter was oblique, as is usual in *Rhabditis*. The tail was conoid to the middle, and thence to the hair-like terminus narrow. For further information consult Pl. III.

Hab.—In humus about the roots of banana plants, Fiji, July, 1891.

6. **Rhabditis** sp. (?). $\frac{3 \cdot \quad 15 \cdot 6 \quad 22 \cdot 6 \quad 7 \quad 65 \cdot 6}{1 \cdot 9 \quad 3 \cdot 2 \quad 3 \cdot 4 \quad 3 \cdot 4 \quad 2}$ ·5 mm. Young worms having the foregoing dimensions were abundant between the sheaths of diseased banana plants sent from Fiji, July, 1891. The cuticula was traversed by numerous transverse striæ. The neck was conoid, the head truncate. There were six low lips on which no papillæ could be seen. The prismoid pharynx was one-eighth as wide as long. The anterior part of the œsophagus was one-half as wide as the neck, and to it succeeded an ellipsoidal median bulb, nearly two-thirds as wide as the neck; thence to the posterior bulb, which was of about the same size and shape as the median, the œsophagus was not above one-fourth as wide as the neck. The intestine was over two-thirds as wide as the body. The tail was conical. Further details with regard to this species will be found on Pl. III.

Genus MONHYSTERA, Bastian.

M. rustica, Bütschli. $\frac{\cdot 7 \quad 7 \quad 10 \cdot \quad \cdot 57^{\cdot 20} \quad 75 \cdot}{2 \cdot 2 \quad 1 \quad 4 \cdot \quad 4\frac{1}{2} \quad 2\frac{1}{2}}$ ·42 mm. The cuticle seems destitute of striæ. The nearly cylindroid neck terminates in a truncate head bearing near its margin six spreading setæ, arising opposite the base of the pharynx, each one-fourth as long as the head is wide. There are six (?) indistinct papillæ inside the row of setæ. The circular lateral organs are one-fourth as wide as the neck, and are placed at a distance from the anterior extremity equal to four times the depth of the simple somewhat cup-shaped pharynx. This latter is one-third as wide as the head and leads into a cylindroid œsophagus nearly two-thirds as wide as the neck and presenting a very slight expansion in front of the distinct and deep cardiac constriction. For some distance behind the pharynx the œsophagus is very transparent. The lining of the œsophagus when seen in optical section is more or less sinuous. At the beginning, that is opposite the cardia, the intestine is somewhat transparent, giving rise at first to the impression that some gland-like organ is present here, but careful examination serves to dispel the deception. The intestine is two-thirds as wide as the body and is composed of cells indistinctly to be seen on account of the multitude of granules with which they are filled. The transparent rectum is conoid, and its length is equal to that of the anal body-diameter. Nothing was learned concerning either the ventral excretory organs or the lateral fields. The nerve-ring is situated near the middle of the neck. The tail is conoid to the terminus, where it is one-sixth as wide as at the base. The vulva is depressed. The eggs are twice as long as the body is wide and one-fourth as wide as long, and are probably deposited before segmentation begins. Illustrations on Pl. ii.

Hab.—Found in humus about the roots of banana plants, Fiji, July, 1891, where it appeared to be uncommon. It is found also in Western Europe and many parts of Australia.

Genus TRIPYLA, Bastian.

The comparatively simple and rudimentary Nematodes composing this genus have the proportions indicated by the generic formulæ $\frac{.0 \quad .7 \quad 10 \cdot \quad \cdot 55^{.73} \quad 96 \cdot}{1\cdot6 \quad 1 \quad 3\cdot2 \quad 3\cdot6 \quad 2\cdot7}$ 2 mm. and $\frac{.0 \quad 6\cdot8 \quad 19 \cdot \quad -M- \quad 86 \cdot}{1\cdot6 \quad 2\cdot8 \quad 3\cdot3 \quad 3\cdot5 \quad 2\cdot7}$ 2 mm. The species are usually found in moist or muddy soil, though one is marine. The cuticle is in most cases finely striated and destitute of any conspicuous hairs except the cephalic setæ, which apparently vary in number from six to ten and are invariably situated on the margin of the head, being in some cases so reduced in size as to resemble papillæ. The conoid neck ends in a head usually truncate and bearing three broad flat and inconspicuous lips armed with one or more inconspicuous papillæ. Nothing is known concerning the lateral organs ; they must if present be very inconspicuous. There are no eye-spots. A pharynx is altogether absent, the mouth opening being on the surface of the head. The conoid to cylindroid œsophagus is sometimes slightly larger near the head ; it is separated from the intestine, which is one-half to three-fourths as wide as the body, by a distinct constriction. The junction of the œsophagus with the intestine often forms a flat bulb-like structure—pseudo-bulb. The rectum is short, seldom exceeding in length the anal body-diameter. Little is known concerning the ventral excretory gland; traces of it have been observed in but one species. In this respect, as well as in many others, this genus resembles *Monhystera*. The nerve-ring encircles the œsophagus squarely some distance in front of the middle of the neck. The tail has the same shape in both sexes, namely, conoid from the inconspicuous anus; the terminus, which is invariably a trifle swollen and often mucronate, gives exit to the secretions of the caudal glands,—always present. The female sexual organs are commonly double and symmetrically reflexed. What little evidence there is points toward the number of testicles being two (—M—). A ventral row of equidistant accessory sexual organs occurs on the male and extends forward from the anus sometimes to near the head. The two equal cuneiform spicula are straight or slightly curved and seldom exceed the anal body-diameter in length; they are accompanied by small accessory pieces. There is no bursa. Probably only a discovery of the males of the species *monhystera* (and possibly also of *arenicola*) can determine whether that species is really a member of this genus.

KEY TO TRIPYLA.

Cephalic setæ none, *i.e.*, reduced to papillæ.
    Length about 3· mm., head rounded.
        Striæ coarse and conspicuous.. 1. *salsa.*
        Striæ fine and inconspicuous.. 2. *papillata.*
    Length 1·4 mm. to 2·5 mm., head truncate.
        When 1·4 mm. long read.. 3. *affinis.*
        When 2·5 m.m. long read.. 4. *glomerans.*
Cephalic setæ present, not reduced to papillæ.
    Female sexual organs asymmetrical.
        Vulva 64 %, tail 5 %.. { 5. *arenicola.* 6. *minor.*
        Vulva 78 %, tail 9 %... 7. *monhystera.*
    Female sexual organs symmetrical.
        Habitat marine .... 8. *marina.*
        Habitat not marine.
            Œsophagus 25 %.. 9. *intermedia.*
            Œsophagus little, if any, exceeding 20 %.
                Tail occupying about 20 % of the length, conoid........................... 10. *filicaudata.*
                Tail occupying about 15 % of the length, conoid....................... 11. *setifera.*
                Tail occupying about 10 % of the length, anterior half only conoid... 12. *tenuicauda.*

KEY TO THE MALES.

Spicula shorter than the anal body-diameter.
    Habitat marine... 8. *marina.*
    Habitat not marine.. 11. *setifera.*

Spicula longer than the anal body-diameter.......... .... 12. *tenuicauda.*
Spicula about equalling the anal body-diameter in length.
    Setæ none.
        Anterior extremity rounded.. 2. *papillata*
        Anterior extremity truncate.
            Accessory pieces one-fourth as long as spicula.................................... 4. *glomerans.*
            Accessory pieces rudimentary... 3. *affinis.*
    Setæ 6... 10. *filicaudata.*

Or,

Setæ 6-10.
    Habitat marine... 6. *marina.*
    Habitat not marine.
        Spicula as long as the anal body-diameter, tail 22 %......... .... 10. *filicaudata.*
        Spicula longer than the anal body-diameter, tail 9 %... .... 12. *tenuicauda.*
        Spicula shorter than the anal body-diameter, tail 16 %...................... .... 11. *setifera.*
Setæ none.
    Accessory pieces one-fourth as long as the spicula .... 4. *glomerans.*
    Accessory pieces rudimentary.
        Length 3·2 mm., head rather rounded.. 2. *papillata.*
        Length 1·4 mm., head truncate.. 3. *affinis.*

1. T. salsa, Bastian. $\frac{0 \quad ? \quad 17 \cdot \quad '50 \cdot \quad 87 \cdot}{17 \quad ? \quad 32 \quad 38 \quad 22}$ ₃·₁₇mm. The cuticle is marked by about three hundred and fifty transverse striæ. The head is rounded in front and bears two lateral papillæ. The œsophagus is cylindrical; the intestine is three-fifths as wide as the body; rectum half as long as the anal body-diameter. The junction of the œsophagus with the intestine is such as to give rise to the appearance of a "collar" or pseudo-bulb. The lateral fields are one-fifth as wide as the body. Terminus one-sixth as wide as the base of the tail. Male unknown.

Hab.—Found on roots of *Ruppia maritima*, in brackish water, England.

2. T. papillata, Bütschli. $\frac{0 \cdot \quad 67 \quad 18 \cdot \quad '55 \cdot^{25} \quad 86 \cdot}{16 \quad 24 \quad 27 \quad 28 \quad 21}$ ₃·₂ mm. Cuticula striated; head rounded in front, bearing three rows of papillæ, of which one represents the row of cephalic setæ; œsophagus conoid, anteriorly less but posteriorly more, than one-half as wide as the corresponding part of the neck; cardiac constriction exceedingly deep; tessellated intestine at first only one-fourth as wide as the body; rectum half as long as the anal body-diameter; juncture of the œsophagus with the intestine such that a very oblate pseudo-bulb is formed; terminus one-sixth as wide as the base of the tail; eggs as long as the body is wide; ovaries reaching about half-way back to the vulva. $\frac{0 \cdot \quad 7 \cdot \quad 18 \cdot \quad M \quad 83 \cdot}{16 \quad 24 \quad 27 \quad 28 \quad 21}$ ₃·₂ mm. Spicula equalling in length the anal body-diameter, with a central stiffening piece; accessory pieces rudimentary.

E

Hab.—Mud and moist earth, and among confervæ, Holland, and Frankfort, Germany.

3. **T. affinis,** de Man. $\frac{0 \cdot\ \ 8 \cdot\ \ 19 \cdot\ \ \cdot52 \cdot^{90}\ \ 83 \cdot}{2 \cdot\ \ 3 \cdot\ \ 8 \cdot 8\ \ 4 \cdot 1\ \ 2 \cdot 9}$ 1·4 mm. Cuticle marked by about four hundred transverse striæ; cephalic papillæ in three rows of six each, the middle row largest and representing the setæ; œsophagus conoid, in its narrowest part less than half as wide as the neck, with a distinct cephalic swelling; intestine tessellated, nearly two-thirds as wide as the body; rectum equalling the anal body-diameter in length; juncture of the œsophagus with the intestine forming a bulb-like swelling; terminus one-fifth as wide as the base of the tail; vagina half as long as the body is wide; eggs one and one-half times as long as the body is wide, and one-third as wide as long; ovaries extending two-thirds of the way back to the vulva. $\frac{0 \cdot\ \ 9 \cdot\ \ 19 \cdot\ \ M\ \ 83 \cdot}{2 \cdot\ \ 3 \cdot\ \ 3 \cdot 8\ \ 4 \cdot 1\ \ 2 \cdot 9}$ 1·4 mm. A ventral row of fourteen equidistant accessory organs extend from the anus to near the mouth; spicula elongated-cuneiform, nearly straight, rather acute, equal in length to the anal body-diameter; accessory pieces rudimentary.

Hab.—Found in moist marshes and meadows, Holland.

4. **T. glomerans,** Bastian. Female unknown. $\frac{0 \cdot\ \ ?\ \ 21 \cdot\ \ M\ \ 86 \cdot}{1 \cdot 3\ \ ?\ \ 4 \cdot 3\ \ 4 \cdot 8\ \ 3 \cdot}$ 2·9 mm. Cuticle traversed by about six hundred and eighty transverse striæ; œsophagus cylindroid, half as wide as the neck; intestine three-fifths as wide as the body; pseudo-bulb flat; terminus one-seventh as wide as the base of the tail; spicula arcuate-cuneiform, slightly exceeding the anal body-diameter in length; accessory pieces one-fourth as long as the spicula.

Hab.—Mud of ponds, England.

5. **T. arenicola,** de Man. $\frac{0 \cdot\ \ ?\ \ 17 \cdot\ \ \cdot64 \cdot^{18}\ \ 95 \cdot}{2 \cdot\ \ ?\ \ 3 \cdot\ \ 3 \cdot 8\ \ 3 \cdot 4}$ 1·4 mm. Cuticle smooth; head truncate, bearing ten setæ arranged as usual, the submedian pairs unequal, the larger ones being half as long as the head is wide and very stout and acute; lips with a row of small papillæ in front of the setæ; œsophagus conoid, anteriorly one-third, but posteriorly one-half, as wide as the neck; intestine two-thirds as wide as the body, without distinct tessellation; rectum exceeding the anal body-diameter in length; pseudo-bulb present; tail ventrally arcuate; terminus narrow, rounded, mucronate; this and the following distinguished from the remaining species by the asymmetrical female sexual organs; ovary reaching three-fourths the way back to the vulva. Male unknown.

Hab.—Found in Holland.

6. **T. minor,** n.sp. $\frac{\cdot7\ \ 8 \cdot 3\ \ 20 \cdot\ \ \cdot68 \cdot^{26}\ \ 94 \cdot}{2 \cdot 5\ \ 3 \cdot 4\ \ 3 \cdot 6\ \ 3 \cdot 6\ \ 2 \cdot 2}$ 1·2 mm. Cuticle apparently without markings; hairs minute, if any; neck cylindroid; head truncate, bearing on its outer margin ten

spreading setæ arranged in the usual manner, four, *i.e.*, one of each submedian pair, being half as long as the others, these latter measuring one-half as long as the head is wide; lips three, each with two papillæ; lateral organs probably represented by small elliptical markings no wider than the base of the cephalic setæ and situated at a distance from the anterior extremity nearly equal to the width of the head; eyes none; pharynx infundibuliform, simple; œsophagus sub-cylindrical, one-third to three-fifths as wide as the neck, widest at the pharynx and posteriorly; cardiac collum distinct; intestine three-fourths as wide as the body, loosely granular and quite transparent; rectum two-thirds as long as the anal body-diameter; no ventral gland seen; nerve-ring encircling the œsophagus squarely, half as wide as the œsophagus at the point encircled; body diminishing suddenly in size near the anus; tail conoid to the middle, where it is one-third as wide as at the anus, thence more or less cylindroid to the conoid terminus, which contains a small outlet for the secretion of the caudal glands; anus depressed, more or less open; vulva not very prominent; eggs three to four times as long as the body is wide and one-fourth as wide as long; reflexed portion of the ovary reaching nearly to the vulva. Several drawings of this little worm will be found on Pl. iv.

Hab.—Soil about banana plants, Fiji, July, 1891.

7. **T. monhystera,** de Man. $\frac{0 \cdot\ \ ?\ \ 20 \cdot\ \ -78 \cdot\ \ 94 \cdot}{13\ \ ?\ \ 2 \cdot\ \ 2 \cdot\ \ 17}$ 1·8 mm. The smooth cuticle bears four sub-cephalic setæ behind the six slender cephalic setæ, the latter being half as long as the head is wide. The truncate head bears papillæ round the mouth. Lateral organs are perhaps present. The conoid œsophagus, which is a trifle enlarged in the anterior fourth, is posteriorly one-half, though anteriorly one-third, as wide as the neck. The intestine is three-fourths as wide as the body and ends in a rectum about as long as the anal body-diameter. The terminus is very narrow, but mucronate. The eggs are over three times as long as the body is wide and one-fifth as wide as long. The male is unknown.

Hab.—Marshy places, on the roots of plants, Holland, not common.

8. **T. marina,** Bütschli. $\frac{0 \cdot\ \ ?\ \ 16 \cdot\ \ 50 \cdot\ \ 90 \cdot}{23\ \ ?\ \ 39\ \ 42\ \ 36}$ 1·6 mm. Cuticle smooth; cephalic setæ six, nearly one-third as long as the head is wide; lumen or lining of the œsophagus widened behind the mouth; intestine half as wide as the body, thin-walled, with a large cardiac cavity; lateral, median and submedian fields present, the first perhaps half as wide as the body; anterior two-thirds of the tail convex-conoid, thence having a uniform diameter one-fifth as great as at the base; $\frac{0 \cdot\ \ ?\ \ 16 \cdot\ \ M\ \ 98 \cdot}{23\ \ ?\ \ 39\ \ ?\ \ 36}$ 1·6 mm. Spicula cuneiform, three-fifths as long as the anal body-diameter, slightly bent near the middle; accessory pieces small, quadrangular.

Hab.—Strand, Kiel, Germany. Perhaps not a *Tripyla*.

9. **T. intermedia**, Bütschli. $\frac{0\cdot}{1\cdot6}\frac{7}{7}\frac{25\cdot}{8\cdot9}\frac{'53\cdot^{28}}{4\cdot}\frac{84\cdot}{3\cdot}$ 1·mm. Head truncate, with six cephalic setæ, each about one-fourth as long as the head is wide, with a row of papillæ inside the setæ; œsophagus conoid, half as wide as the neck; intestine at once two-thirds as wide as the body; rectum half as long as the anal body-diameter; pseudo-bulb present, irregular; vulva very prominent.

Hab.—Roots of grass, Frankfort-on-the-Main, Germany.

10. **T. filicaudata**, de Man. $\frac{0\cdot}{1\cdot5}\frac{7}{7}\frac{18\cdot}{2\cdot4}\frac{'46\cdot^{30}}{2\cdot8}\frac{78\cdot}{1\cdot9}$ 2·mm. About eight hundred transverse striæ traverse the cuticula. The truncate head bears four submedian sub-cephalic setæ just behind the six stout acute cephalic setæ (the latter one-third as long as the head is wide), and two rows of papillæ round the mouth. The œsophagus is nearly cylindrical, being only slightly narrower in the middle than elsewhere. The tessellated intestine ends in a rectum two-thirds as long as the anal body-diameter. Pseudo-bulb present. The lateral fields are one-third as wide as the body. The tail is usually ventrally arcuate and ends in a terminus one-seventh as wide as its base. The vulva is prominent and projecting. The eggs are nearly as wide as the body and twice as long as wide. The ovaries extend one-third the distance back to the vulva. $\frac{0\cdot}{1\cdot6}\frac{7}{7}\frac{20\cdot}{2\cdot4}\frac{M}{2\cdot6}\frac{78\cdot}{1\cdot9}$ 1·7mm. Fourteen or fifteen accessory organs form a ventral row reaching from the anus to near the mouth. The nearly straight cuneiform spicula equal the anal body-diameter in length and are stiffened by central pieces of chitin. There are no accessory pieces.

Hab.—Found in moist earth, Holland; not common.

11. **T. setifera**, Bütschli. $\frac{0\cdot}{2\cdot}\frac{7}{7}\frac{20\cdot}{3\cdot}\frac{'57\cdot^{31}}{3\cdot6}\frac{84\cdot}{2\cdot6}$ 1·7mm. Cuticle finely striated; head truncate, with six cephalic setæ, each nearly half as long as the head is wide, and a row of papillæ both inside and outside these setæ; œsophagus conoid, anteriorly one-half, but posteriorly two-thirds as wide as the neck, hardly enlarged anteriorly; intestine tessellated, two-thirds as wide as the body; rectum nearly equalling the anal body-diameter in length; pseudo-bulb present; terminus one-fifth as wide as the base of the tail; vulva projecting; ovaries reaching nearly back to the vulva. $\frac{0\cdot}{3\cdot}\frac{7}{7}\frac{21\cdot}{3\cdot5}\frac{-M-}{3\cdot9}\frac{84\cdot}{3\cdot4}$ 1·7mm. Row of ventral accessory male organs extending forward to near the mouth; spicula arcuate-cuneiform with a central stiffening piece, four-fifths as long as the anal body-diameter; accessory pieces rudimentary; blind end of the anterior testicle lying near the commencement of the middle third of the body.

Hab.—Marshy earth, Holland; roots of a fungus, Germany.

12. **T. tenuicauda**, n.sp. Female unknown. $\frac{0\cdot}{1\cdot2}\frac{5\cdot}{2\cdot4}\frac{17\cdot}{2\cdot8}\frac{M}{2\cdot6}\frac{91\cdot}{1\cdot7}$ 2·5mm. The cuticle is smooth and bears very short papilla-like hairs throughout. The neck is rather convex-

conoid, especially anteriorly, where it ends in a rounded head which is truncate at the mouth. There are ten cephalic setæ arranged as usual, one of each of the submedian pairs being shorter, the others being about one-sixth as long as the head is wide. I could discover no papillæ. The conoid œsophagus is anteriorly one-half, posteriorly three-fifths as wide as the neck, being only very slightly enlarged near the head ; its lining is not very distinctly to be seen. From the rather indistinct cardiac collum the intestine is at once three-fourths as wide as the body. The duct of the ventral gland ends in an ellipsoidal ampulla, and empties through a ventral pore at the commencement of the second fifth of the neck (3·6%). The lateral fields are one-fourth as wide as the body. The anterior half of the tail is concave-conoid, thence, however, it is uniformly one-fifteenth as wide as at the base. The three small elongated pyriform caudal glands lie just behind the anus. The ventral row of male accessory sexual organs is composed of *seven fascicles* equidistantly arranged, the posterior one being opposite the middle of the spicula and the whole row being considerably longer than the tail (14°/₀). The elongated spicula are of nearly uniform size, being slightly arcuate in the proximal halves ; their length is half as great again as that of the anal body-diameter. There are probably two testicles arranged symmetrically.

Hab.—Mud of a brook, Sydney, New South Wales, Australia.

Genus PRISMATOLAIMUS, de Man.

1. P. **intermedius**, Bütschli (?). $\frac{2 \cdot 2}{5}\ \frac{1}{1}\ \frac{27 \cdot}{3 \cdot}\ \frac{\cdot 71 \cdot^{30}}{2\frac{1}{4}}\ \frac{76 \cdot 5\,(?)}{19}$ ·5 mm. The cuticle is traversed by about four hundred transverse striæ. Minute and extremely inconspicuous hairs occur from place to place throughout the length of the body. The conoid neck terminates anteriorly in a truncate head, bearing near its margin six equal spreading setæ, each about two-thirds as long as the head is wide. The lips are low and indistinct, but appear to be three in number; they bore no papillæ that I could see. Neither eyes nor lateral organs were to be seen. The edges of the triquetrous pharynx are indicated by three longitudinal ribs ; the main part is two-fifths as wide as the head and this is continued by a diminishing part through which it is connected with the œsophageal lumen. The œsophagus where it receives the pharynx is two-thirds as wide as the corresponding part of the neck; it soon diminishes however to one-half as wide as the neck, then gradually widens posteriorly until it becomes two-thirds as wide as the base of the neck. The granular intestine, which is two-fifths as wide as the body, is separated from the œsophagus by a deep, broad and very distinct constriction, opposite to which are two bodies whose function is unknown to me. I discovered nothing concerning the ventral gland, the longitudinal fields or

the nerve-ring. The cinctured tail is conoid to the terminus, where it is one-fifth as wide as at the anus. There appear to be no caudal glands. The eggs are two-thirds as long as the body is wide and two-thirds as wide as long. The reflexed portion of the ovary reaches two-fifths the way back to the vulva and contains upwards of a dozen developing ova which in the distal part are arranged in several rows. The male has not yet been seen. I have made a number of sketches of the anatomy of this species ; these are reproduced on Pl. iv.

Hab.—Soil about banana plants, Fiji, 1891, not common. I am not positive that this worm is the same as that first seen by Prof. Bütschli in Germany ; however the resemblance is so great that I do not feel justified in applying a new name, especially as the male has yet to be seen.

2. **P. australis**, n.sp. $\frac{1\cdot2}{1\cdot5} \frac{7}{2\cdot1} \frac{21\cdot}{2\cdot3} \frac{\cdot41''}{2\cdot4} \frac{68\cdot}{1\cdot5}$, 1·mm. The plain transverse striæ of the cuticle are easily resolvable with a moderate power. The hairs, which occur throughout the length of the animal, are very inconspicuous except on the tail. The cylindroid neck terminates in a truncate head bearing ten setæ, each about half as long as the head is wide and arranged as usual, the members of the submedian pairs being subequal. The larger of the cephalic setæ just mentioned are of peculiar form, the diameter of the hair suddenly decreasing near the tip, the effect being that the hair appears as if encased in a sheath. There are papillæ round the mouth. Small lateral organs appear to me to be placed about as far behind the base of the pharynx as the latter is behind the anterior extremity. Their nature I could not make out. The short prismoid pharynx is nearly half as wide as the head and is covered over by the lips. The cylindroid œsophagus is half as wide as the neck. The thick-walled granular intestine is two-thirds as wide as the body and is separated from the œsophagus by a distinct and deep constriction. The cardia is transparent and gives rise to a pseudo-bulb. The tail is conoid from the depressed anus but tapers more rapidly at first than towards the end. It appeared that tail glands were present, the terminus being narrow but convex-conoid as if furnishing an outlet for the secretion of caudal glands, and on that account such glands may be supposed to be present, though not seen. The eggs are two-thirds as wide as the body, and five times as long as wide, and are probably deposited before segmentation begins.

Hab.—Roots of plants, Moss Vale, New South Wales, Australia.

Genus PLECTUS, Bastian.

P. insignis, n.sp. $\frac{4\cdot6}{2\cdot6} \frac{15\cdot}{3\cdot} \frac{26\cdot}{4\cdot2} \frac{49\cdot}{4\cdot2} \frac{87\cdot}{2\cdot7}$, ·66 mm. The cuticle is traversed by plain transverse striæ easily made out with a lens of medium power. Short hairs occur throughout the length of the worm. The neck is conoid,—somewhat convex conoid near the truncate head. Half-way between the anterior extremity and the lateral organs occur six cephalic setæ, each one-third as long as the head is wide. The obscure lips are probably three in number. The lateral organs are unclosed circumferences, one-fourth as wide as the head, and are situated opposite the middle of the pharynx; regarded as spirals, the right is a left-handed spiral, and the left a right-handed spiral. The long two-chambered pharynx reaches half-way to the nerve-ring, only the anterior part being referred to in the above formula: the anterior half is a strongly-lined tube, wider at the mouth, namely, one-third as wide as the head; the posterior half somewhat resembles the remainder of the œsophageal tube. This latter is anteriorly one-third as wide as the neck, but posteriorly narrows to one-fourth as wide as the neck, and finally expands to form an elongated bulb three-fourths as wide as the base of the neck and containing a distinct valve. The transparent intestine, which is two-thirds as wide as the body and rather thin-walled, is separated from the œsophagus by a distinct constriction. The ventral excretory pore is situated opposite the oblique nerve-ring. The two wings of the cuticle found on each side of the body are separated from each other by a distance equal to one-seventh the diameter of the body. The tail is conoid and ends in an apiculate terminus one-third as wide as the anal body-diameter is long. Caudal glands as in other *Plecti.* The vulva is inconspicuous. The eggs are three-fourths as wide as the body and five times as long as wide; only one seen and that behind the vulva, unsegmented. The female sexual apparatus is possibly single and reflexed, extending first forward and then back past the vulva.

Hab.—About the roots of plants, Moss Vale, New South Wales, Australia.

Genus CEPHALOBUS, Bastian.

1. **C. similis, n.sp.** Very likely a new genus may have to be created to receive this interesting little worm, which I found on lettuce from a Chinaman's garden. The only specimen seen, a young female, gave the following dimensions: $\frac{1\cdot6 \quad 15\cdot5 \quad 22\cdot4 \quad 51\cdot \quad 86\cdot}{5\cdot3 \quad 44 \quad 47 \quad 5\cdot6 \quad 2\cdot8}$ ·84 mm. Neck conoid; head truncate, bearing six large bluntly conical lips; pharynx deep and complicated, composed of three parts as follows: 1, the part alluded to in the formula as 1·6 % deep, one-third as wide as the head, fully twice as deep as wide, tapering behind into 2, which is closed and surrounded with a separate muscular layer, but which however has not so great a diameter as 3, which is nearly twice as long as the two anterior parts taken together, more than half as wide as the corresponding part of the neck and contains a narrow elongated cavity in its anterior half; œsophagus of three parts, with the pharynx forming a structure of the same form as the œsophagus of *Rhabditis, i.e.,* the anterior three-fifths about half as wide as the neck and connected with the rather weak ellipsoidal cardiac bulb

by a tube one-fourth as wide as the part of the neck it traverses; ventral excretory pore opposite the nerve-ring ; intestine thick-walled, with a distinct chitinous lining ; rectum as long as the anal body-diameter; tail conical; vulva elevated; female sexual organs probably double and symmetrical.

Hab.—Lettuce, Sydney, N.S.W., Australia.

2. **O. infestans,** n.sp. Female unknown. $\frac{2\cdot7\ \ 15\cdot\ \ 23\cdot\ \ '_{M}{}^{56}\ \ 92\cdot}{2\cdot\ \ 8\cdot9\ \ 4\cdot4\ \ 4\cdot5\ \ 3\cdot}$ ·62 mm. The cuticle is not striated and is destitute of hairs. The conoid neck ends in a small truncate head with a slightly expanded lip-region. Neither setæ nor papillæ were seen on the head. The anterior half of the pharynx is triquetrous and about one-fourth as wide as the head, while the posterior half is much narrower. The cylindrical anterior half of the œsophagus is about one-third as wide as the corresponding part of the neck ; the posterior half is at first very slender, less than half as wide as in the anterior part, but expands finally to form an ellipsoidal bulb half as wide as the base of the neck. There are no eyes. The intestine is three-fourths as wide as the body. The tail is conoid. The length of the two equal elongated arcuate acute spicula is equal to that of the anal body-diameter ; the proximæ are cephalated by constriction. The two accessory pieces are more than half as long as the spicula and are arranged parallel to them. At least four pairs of submedian papillæ occur on the posterior part of the male: 1, a pair as far in front of the spicula as the heads of the latter are in front of the anus ; 2, a pair opposite the anus ; 3, a pair at the beginning of the central third of the tail ; 4, a pair at the end of the second third of the tail, *i.e.*, as far behind the anus as the pre-anal pair is in front of it. The blind end of the single reflexed testicle lies as far behind the cardia as the latter is behind the lips ; from thence it passes forward half-way to the cardia, then turns backward. The ejaculatory duct appears to be twice as long as the tail. Sketches of this worm occur on Pl. IV.

Hab.—Found in great numbers (young) among the sheaths of diseased banana plants, Fiji, July, 1891.

Genus AULOLAIMUS, de Man.

A. exilis, n.sp. $\frac{4\cdot5\ \ 7\cdot5\ \ 23\cdot\ \ -46\cdot{}^{14}\ \ 73\cdot}{1\cdot6\ \ 1\cdot9\ \ 2\cdot1\ \ 2\cdot\ \ 1\cdot}$ 1·07 mm. I place this worm with some hesitation in Dr. de Man's genus *Aulolaimus* for reasons that will be plain on comparing the Fiji worm with that of Holland. The cuticle appeared to me entirely naked and destitute of striæ. The sub-cylindroid neck terminates in a convex-conoid head, whose truncate apex bears three (?) obscure lips without conspicuous papillæ. There are no eyes, and no lateral organs were seen. The cylindroid pharynx is on the average one-fourth as wide as the head, and is continued as a lumen half as wide in the œsophagus proper. This latter is cylindroidal and a little more than half as wide as the neck. A rather weak cardiac bulb appears to exist ; the cardiac collum and the bulb were less distinctly seen than would appear from the figures. The granular intestine is two-thirds as wide as the body. I discovered nothing concerning the ventral gland. The nerve-ring, which is placed far forward, makes but a slight angle with the œsophagus. The slightly ventrally arcuate tail is conoid in the anterior third, and thence is setaceous to the terminus, whose structure precludes its being the outlet of caudal glands ; these latter, therefore, probably do not exist. The eggs are apparently as long as the body is wide and two-thirds as wide as long. Male not seen. Sketches of this worm occur on Pl. II.

Hab.—Found in soil about banana plants, Fiji, July, 1891 ; not common.

Genus DORYLAIMUS, Bastian.

1. **D. exilis**, n.sp. $\frac{.3 \quad 6\cdot3 \quad 26\cdot9 \quad \cdot 55\cdot^{.25} \quad 91\cdot4}{1\cdot \quad 2\cdot \quad 2\cdot2 \quad 2\cdot4 \quad 1\cdot3}$ 176 mm. No cuticular markings were noted on the two specimens examined. The neck retains the diameter of the body in the greater part of its length, but becomes convex-conoid in the anterior fourth. The truncate head bears six distinct lips, each of which is armed with the usual two papillæ ; the lip-region is expanded and conspicuous. The well-developed spear slides in a close-fitting collar situated just behind the lip-region. The anterior part of the œsophagus is one-third as wide as the corresponding part of the neck ; the expansion takes place rather suddenly somewhat in front of the middle, and thence to the intestine the œsophagus is nearly three-fourths as wide as the body, its central canal being unusually conspicuous on account of the refractive nature of its thick chitinous lining. The cardiac collum is very distinct. The somewhat dark-coloured intestine is three-fifths as wide as the body and is rather thick-walled. The narrow rectum is nearly twice as long as the anal body-diameter. The pre-rectal portion of the intestine is twice as long as the rectum. The tail is conoid, but diminishes more rapidly in the anterior fourth than elsewhere. The eggs are two and one-half times as long as the body is wide and about one-third as wide as long. $\frac{.4 \quad 7\cdot \quad 20\cdot \quad -M-^{.25} \quad 98\cdot5}{1\cdot \quad 2\cdot2 \quad 2\cdot4 \quad 2\cdot7 \quad 2\cdot}$ 1·6 to 2 mm. I have little doubt that this is the male of this species, although I did not find the two sexes associated. The differences in structure are very slight, if any ; possibly the pre-rectal portion of the intestine is a trifle longer in these males. The male tail is blunt and rounded, hemispherical-conoid, and about four (possibly more) papillæ are found upon it near the end, to which nerves are plainly seen to pass. A ventral row of about sixteen closely approximated innervated papillæ begins at a distance in front of the spicula equal to the length of the latter and extends forward to some-

F

what behind the anterior end of the pre-rectal portion of the intestine. Oblique copulatory lateral muscles occur, co-extensive with the pre-rectum. The elongated acute spicula are bent at the middle ; their length is one and one-third times that of the anal body-diameter. Figured on Pl. v.

Hab.—Somewhat rare about the roots of banana plants in Fiji, July, 1891.

2. **D. obtusus**, n.sp. $\frac{4\cdot\ 6\cdot\ 24\cdot\ 42\cdot\ 68\cdot4}{4\cdot\ 2\cdot\ 27\ 28\ 19}$ 1·62 mm. The transparent cuticle of this rather striking species is finely striated. The slightly convex-conoid neck terminates in a somewhat truncate head with six inconspicuous lips each bearing two papillæ in the usual position. The anterior part of the œsophagus is one-third as wide as the corresponding part of the neck and ends in a well developed spear; the posterior part, beginning suddenly somewhat in front of the middle, is fully twice as wide as the anterior part. The cardiac collum is distinct but not deep. The intestine is about two-thirds as wide as the body and the contents of its component cells are sometimes so arranged as to give it an irregularly segmented appearance. The rectum is about three-fourths as long as the anal body-diameter, while the pre-rectal portion of the intestine is from three to four times as long as the rectum. The tail is short and rounded, the cuticula being slightly thicker in the terminal part. Figured on Pl. v.

Hab.—Common about the roots of banana plants, in Fiji, July, 1891. Notwithstanding careful search, no males were found. The females did not seem very active.

3. **D. longicollis**, n.sp. $\frac{4\ 64\ 87\cdot\ 48\cdot48\ 99\cdot}{8\ 42\ 86\ 36\ 2}$ 2·96 mm. No markings were observed on the smooth and rather thick transparent cuticula. The neck is conoid and ends in a rounded head composed of two parts of about equal length, of which the anterior is much the narrower, and bears six quite rudimentary lips. Cephalic papillæ if present must be so inconspicuous as to have escaped careful search. The well developed spear is about as long as the head is wide and about one-ninth as wide as the head. The sinuous anterior third of the unusually long œsophagus is one-fourth as wide as the corresponding part of the neck ; at the end of the anterior third the œsophagus becomes suddenly muscular and larger, that is to say, one-half as wide as the neck, and continues thus to the end where it is separated from the intestine by a distinct collum. In young specimens the œsophagus occupies more than half of the length of the body. The thin-walled intestine is two-thirds as wide as the body, its component cells being of such a size that about twelve side by side make up the circumference, and having their granular contents so disposed as to give rise to a rather distinct tessellation. The rectum equals the anal body-diameter in length. In young worms the pre-rectal portion of the intestine was about twice as long as the rectum ; presumably the ratio is no greater in the adults. The lateral fields are

one-fourth as wide as the body. The tail is nearly hemispherical. From the inconspicuous vulva the vagina, which is one-half as long as the body is wide, leads into two long uteri, in either of which the eggs are arranged in several rows. The anterior uterus is so long that the flexure in the oviduct sometimes lies in front of the cardiac region,—something uncommon in free-living nematodes. Supposing the specimens observed to have been mature, the sub-spherical eggs had a diameter one-fourth as great as the diameter of the body. Figured on Pl. vi.

Hab.—The young were common about the roots of banana plants in Fiji, July, 1891. But few adult females were seen, and no males.

4. **D. perfectus, n.sp.** $\frac{4}{1}\frac{7\cdot6}{4}\frac{25\cdot6}{43}\frac{'54'}{'8}\frac{96}{2}$ 2·16 mm. The cuticula is thick and transparent. The neck is conoid, becoming convex-conoid near the head, which is truncate and bears six distinct doubly-papillate lips of the usual form. The well developed spear is one-fifth as wide as the head and slides in a distinct close-fitting collar, situated just behind the lips. The anterior part of the œsophagus is only one-fourth as wide as the corresponding part of the neck, but at the middle it enlarges rather suddenly and becomes two-fifths as wide as the body, its component cells being of such a size that ten side by side make up a circumference, and having their granular contents so disposed as to give rise to a distinct polygonal tessellation. The rectum is twice as long as the anal body-diameter. The pre-rectal portion of the intestine is about four times as long as the anal body-diameter, or in the males, twice as long as the spicula. The intestine is three-fourths as wide as the body. In the neck at least two unicellular glands were observed; each of these was as long as the neck was wide and emptied laterally (or sublaterally) by means of an indistinct ampulla and short narrow distinct chitinous pore which plainly penetrated all the cuticular structures at a distance from the head equal to five per cent. of the length of the body. The vulva is not conspicuous. The eggs are one and one-half times as long as the body is wide, three-fifths as wide as long. $\frac{4}{8}\frac{87}{2\cdot7}\frac{20\cdot3}{3\cdot6}\frac{-M-}{3\cdot6}\frac{35}{8\cdot1}\frac{98\cdot6}{2}$ 2·36 mm. The tail of the male, like that of the female, is rounded, and bears the four sub-median papillæ, also found in the female. A single ventral row of about twenty-three innervated closely approximated low papillæ are found opposite the ductus ejaculatorius, that is to say, begins just in front of the spicula and extends nearly to the anterior extremity of the pre-rectal portion of the intestine. One such papilla stands alone just in front of the anus. Seen in profile the spicula are boomerang-shaped. They are acute, and are stiffened anteriorly by a median thickening. The proximæ are not cephaloid. Accessory pieces are apparently wanting. The spicula are very likely exserted by means of muscles passing obliquely to the extremity of the tail. Oblique copulatory muscles are present throughout the region of the ductus. Figured on Plates v. & vi.

Hab.—The worms were very common in the soil about the roots of banana plants in Fiji, July, 1891. The males were especially common. Only one female was seen, so that I am not perfectly certain that the male and female here described together really belong to one and the same species.

5. **D. granuliferus**, n.sp. $\frac{4}{1\cdot1}\ \frac{8\cdot7}{3\cdot}\ \frac{26\cdot}{3\cdot6}\ \frac{\cdot51\cdot^{62}}{4\cdot8}\ \frac{90\cdot}{2\cdot}$ 1·97mm. The six lips are very distinct and each bears the usual two papillæ. The anterior part of the œsophagus is one-fourth as wide as the corresponding part of the neck and is surrounded in front of the nerve-ring by three elongated granular bodies which become conspicuous when the worm is immersed in weak osmic acid; behind the nerve-ring the œsophagus gradually expands until it becomes, in the posterior half, two-thirds as wide as the neck. The tessellated intestine is about two-thirds as wide as the body and is composed of cells of such a size that about twelve side by side make up the circumference. The narrow rectum is somewhat less than twice as long as the anal body-diameter, being about equal in length to the tail. The pre-rectal portion of the intestine is one and one-half times longer than the rectum. The lateral fields are one-third as wide as the body. The tail is pointed and decreases more rapidly in the anterior half than in the posterior half. The reflexed portions of the ovaries reach half-way back to the vulva. The eggs are a trifle longer than the body is wide and a little more than one-third as wide as long. Figured on Pl. v.

Hab.—Not uncommon about the roots of banana plants in Fiji, July, 1891. No males were found.

6. **D. spiralis**, n.sp. $\frac{\cdot16}{\cdot8}\ \frac{4\cdot4}{2\cdot}\ \frac{15\cdot}{2\cdot2}\ \frac{\cdot45\cdot^{025}}{2\cdot7}\ \frac{99\cdot2}{1\cdot5}$ 5·2mm. The neck is cylindroid to near the nerve-ring; thence it is convex-conoid to the expanded lip-region. There are six distinct lips, and six papillæ, also distinct. The rather slender spear slides in a pharyngeal ring and can be clearly traced back a distance three times as great as the width of the head. The anterior third of the œsophagus is narrow;—it widens rather suddenly, so that the posterior two-thirds are three-fifths as wide as the corresponding part of the neck. The thin-walled tessellated intestine is three-fourths as wide as the body and is composed of cells of such a size that about sixteen are required to build up a circumference. The rectum is as long as the anal body-diameter; the pre-rectum is five times as long as the rectum. The lateral fields are at the neck one-eighth, and at the tail one-fourth, as wide as the body. The conoid-hemispherical tail seems to have a terminal pore and to contain a considerable number of small glands. The depressed vulva leads into a vagina one-half as long as the body is wide. The thick-shelled eggs are more or less ellipsoidal; they are three-fifths as wide as the body and twice as long as wide. The uteri seem to contain but one egg at a time, and this is probably deposited before segmentation begins. The ovaries reach two-thirds to three-fourths the distance back to the vulva. Male unknown.

Hab.—Found among the bases of carrot leaves, Sydney, New South Wales, Australia, in July.

7. **D. domus Glauci,** n.sp. $\frac{.4 \quad 12 \cdot \quad 28 \cdot \quad \cdot 53 \cdot \frac{.43}{.98 \cdot 6}}{1 \cdot \quad 41 \quad 47 \quad 53 \quad 2}$ 1·08 mm. Neck conoid,—convex-conoid anteriorly ; lips six, each with at least one distinct papilla ; spear acute, well developed ; œsophagus at first only one-fifth as wide as the corresponding part of the neck, but gradually and uniformly widening until it is at last more than half as wide as the base of the neck ; rectum nearly twice as long as the anal body-diameter ; pre-rectum three times the length of the rectum, tapering posteriorly ; ovaries reaching two-thirds to three-fourths the way back to the vulva ; eggs thick-shelled, ellipsoidal, as long as the body is wide and over half as wide as long.

Hab.—Found among moss on the walls of the Casa Poetæ, Pompeii, Italy. Possibly the widths given in the formula are too great.

8. **D. Vesuvianus,** n.sp. $\frac{.3 \quad 10 \cdot 5 \quad 20 \cdot \quad \cdot 47 \cdot \frac{.40}{.98 \cdot 3}}{1 \cdot 1 \quad 3 \cdot 2 \quad 3 \cdot 5 \quad 4 \cdot 5 \quad 2 \cdot 3}$ 1·15 mm. In the posterior part the neck is nearly cylindrical, but the anterior third is convex-conoid to the truncate head. The lip-region is not conspicuous, and the lips are either absent or very indistinct. There are perhaps two rows of papillæ, six in each row. The spear is very slender and can be traced backward only for a distance equalling one-fiftieth of the length of the worm. The anterior part of the œsophagus is only about one-fourth as wide as the corresponding part of the neck, but it expands suddenly behind the middle, so that the posterior third (male) or two-fifths (female) is twice as wide, *i.e.,* about half as wide as the base of the neck. The intestine is about half as wide as the body and is marked off from the œsophagus by a distinct constriction. The cardia is broad but not deep. The rectum is only three-fourths as long as the anal body-diameter ; the pre-rectal portion of the intestine, however, is quite as long as the enlarged portion of the œsophagus. The lateral fields are nearly one-third as wide as the body. The tail in either sex is hemispherical or conoid-hemispherical. The inconspicuous vulva leads to a vagina half as long as the body is wide. The reflexed ovaries reach half-way back to the vulva. $\frac{.3 \quad 11 \cdot \quad 25 \cdot \quad -M- \quad 98 \cdot 2}{1 \cdot 3 \quad 3 \cdot 7 \quad 4 \cdot 2 \quad 4 \cdot 5 \quad 2 \cdot 3}$ 1·mm. A ventral row of eleven juxtaposed median innervated papillæ extends forward from opposite the proximal ends of the spicula. These latter are of the usual form and about twice as long as the tail. The internal male sexual organs occupy the posterior two-thirds of the body.

Hab.—Found among moss on the sides of Mount Vesuvius, Italy.

9. **D. labyrinthostoma,** n.sp. $\frac{1 \cdot \quad 7 \cdot \quad 29 \cdot \quad \cdot 50 \cdot \quad 90 \cdot}{1 \cdot 1 \cdot 9 \quad 3 \cdot 2 \quad 2 \cdot 2 \quad 1 \cdot 2}$ 1·75 mm. This species belongs to the group first made known through the researches of Dr. de Man, and characterised by the possession of elaborate mouth parts accessory to the spear. The group represents the acme of development in *Dorylaimus* so far as yet discovered. The spear presents

no very marked contrast with the spear as presented in other groups in the genus. The parts accessory to the spear may conveniently be arranged in two groups, (1) those serving to guide the spear in its forward and backward movements, and (2) those which line the lips and forward part of the pharynx, and serving, in my opinion, to give the animal a firm grip during the operations of piercing and sucking by which it gains its living.   The principal part serving to guide the spear is a chitinous collar which is doubtless a further development of various similar but more simple contrivances found in all nematodes with a pharyngeal spear.   In the present case this collar, which, were it not somewhat too flat, might be called bell-shaped, closely surrounds the spear at the base of the pharynx, being firmly held in place by horny processes anterior to it and partly constituting the interior wall of the pharynx.   The parts lining the lips, and no doubt, as above stated, serving as biting organs, are less easily described.   In the first place it is necessary to note that the lips and the lip-region are constructed externally much as in other *Dorylaimi*: there are six somewhat confluent lips each bearing two papillæ, the lip-region being expanded and the papillæ being arranged in two circles of six each, one circle inside the other but both situated near the margin of the head.   Inside these lips and extending backward some little distance further is the pharynx, which is, roughly speaking, pyriform in shape, with the wider part foremost.   Round the mouth-opening are ranged a number of processes, probably six, one from each lip, which appear to be capable of radial movement.   Opposite the inner and anterior row of labial papillæ a row of numerous longitudinal ribs encircles the anterior part of the pharynx.   The base of these ribs or teeth is a transverse ring larger than any other of its kind found in the head. What appears to be a repetition of this structure on a smaller scale and without the transverse ring occurs slightly further back, that is half-way between the mouth-opening and the spear-guide.   The object of these complex structures is open only to conjecture, but I have little doubt that they are used as biting organs, or possibly as rasping surfaces in tearing down the cells of plants; I do *not* consider them organs of mastication.   The examination of these mouth-parts and a comparison of them with those of *Onyx, Mononchus* and *Oncholaimus,* has convinced me that we have good ground for regarding the spear-bearing genera and what I may call the tooth-bearing genera (represented by *Mononchus, Oncholaimus* and other genera with a distinct dorsal tooth) as being related to each other and perhaps constituting a grand group. The further specific characters of *D. labyrinthostoma* are as follows : cuticle thick, destitute of markings and hairs; neck cylindrical posteriorly, convex-conoid anteriorly; head truncate; lateral organs not seen; eyes none; nerve-ring oblique; œsophagus anteriorly one-fourth as wide as the neck but widening gradually and becoming, near the middle, two-thirds as wide as the neck and so continuing to the end, where it is separated from the intestine by a distinct constriction ; intestine three-fourths as wide as the body, its distinct pre-rectal part being twice as long as the body is wide;

rectum nearly twice as long as the anal body-diameter; tail conical and hair-fine at its terminus, without glands; anus and vulva not conspicuous. Male unknown. Figured on Pl. ii.

Hab.—Soil about banana plants, Fiji, July, 1891, common.

Genus TYLENCHOLAIMUS, de Man.

T. ensiculiferus, n.sp. $\frac{14\cdot4 \quad 7 \quad 29\cdot \quad 34\cdot \quad 98\cdot4}{2\cdot6 \quad 7 \quad 2\cdot0 \quad 9\cdot \quad 2\cdot2}$ 1·75mm. The thick transparent and naked cuticle seems not to be annulated. The neck is cylindroid in the posterior half and convex-conoid in the anterior half. The diameter of the head in the lip-region is equal to ·8 per cent. of the body-length, *i.e.*, is one-third as wide as the base of the spear. The head, somewhat rounded in front, bears no setæ and none but very inconspicuous lips, of which the number is probably three. There are no eyes. No lateral organs were seen. The pharynx, which is half as long and nearly one-third as wide as the neck, contains a spear whose three-bulbed base is one-fourth as wide as the middle of the neck and whose posterior third is three times thicker than the slender anterior two-thirds. From the base of the spear a narrow and, when the spear is not exserted, tortuous canal leads to the muscular much elongated cardiac bulb, which is twice as long as the neck is wide and fully four times as long as wide. The thick-walled granular intestine is one-half as wide as the body and is separated from the cardiac bulb by a deep and distinct constriction; the rectum is one-half as long as the anal body-diameter. The nature of the ventral gland, longitudinal fields, and nerve-ring remain unknown. The posterior end is rounded and thick-skinned, but its internal muscular matter ends in a blunt point. The male was not seen. Drawings of this interesting worm will be found on Pl. vii.

Hab.—Found in soil about the roots of banana plants, Fiji, 1891. Not common.

Genus TYLENCHUS, Bastian.

Transparent striated round worms, in most cases devoid of bristles or setæ, varying in length from one-third of a millimetre to three and a-half millimetres, attacking the tissues of plants, or more rarely animals, by means of a pharyngeal spear and sucking apparatus of the following construction : a three-bulbed spear, capable of being thrust forth and withdrawn by appropriate muscles, is connected with a powerful median œsophageal sucking-bulb by means of a tube whose lining is more chitinous than is usual in other Nematode genera; the median bulb is connected with a smaller posterior bulb of much weaker construction by means of a shorter and weaker tube, which passes through the oblique nerve-ring, situated just behind the median bulb. The posterior bulb may become rudimentary, but probably never quite disappears. Lateral organs as well as visual organs are unknown in the genus. The female sexual apparatus is usually single and asymmetrical, being in that case usually straight and directed forward though often presenting a rudimentary posterior branch, but it may be double and symmetrical. In the former case the vulva is behind the middle; in the latter case it is central. The male possesses two equal slightly arcuate spicula and in most species a more or less well developed bursa.

1. **T. radicicola**, Greef. $\frac{5\cdot2}{4\cdot4} \frac{15\cdot}{3\cdot3} \frac{17\cdot6}{5\cdot4} \frac{Y}{5\cdot6} \frac{87\cdot9}{2\cdot3}$ is the formula for the freshly hatched larva, of which the following is a further description:—Cuticle traversed by about five hundred transverse striæ; neck cylindroid to opposite the base of the buccal cavity, but thence to the mouth is convex-conoid ;

faint indications of lips; three-bulbed spear when at rest drawn back so that its apex is removed half the spear-length from the mouth; ellipsoidal sucking-bulb just in front of the nerve-ring; posterior œsophageal swelling weak and devoid of chitin; intestine pellucid, two-thirds as wide as the body, and having its cells closely packed with granules; ventral excretory pore just opposite the commencement of the intestine; lateral wings occupying an area one-fourth as wide as the body and presenting four parallel lines; tail conical from the inconspicuous anus; caudal glands absent, terminus pointed.

Fig. 4.—Larva of *Tylenchus radicicola.*

I, the larva magnified 190 times. II, head of the same worm magnified 875 times. III, small section of the body magnified 750 times. IV shows at the centre of the circle the actual size of the worm. *s*, spear; *b*, median sucking-bulb; *n*, nerve-ring; *p*, ventral excretory pore; posterior *b*, cardiac bulb; *i*, the intestine; *c*, the cuticle; *l*, the lateral wings of the cuticle.

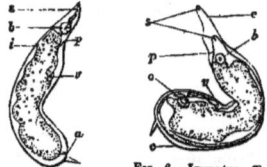

The larvæ, which are found in large numbers in the cavities occupied by the parasitic mother-worms, and also in the surrounding soil, make their way into the rootlets of various plants by means of the special piercing and sucking apparatus, namely, the spear and bulb, and then undergo a remarkable metamorphosis. At an early moult they lose the conical tail and the posterior end becomes rounded. Meanwhile the body, amply nourished by plant-juices, becomes plump, and takes on the dimensions shown in the following formula and the adjacent illustrations : $\frac{4\cdot2}{3\cdot8} \frac{7}{7} \frac{17\cdot9}{9\cdot5} \frac{Y}{16\cdot1} \frac{91\cdot}{6\cdot}$ The larva makes its way into a rootlet by applying its mouth to the surface of the rootlet and exerting a powerful

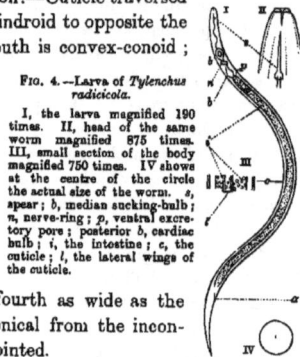

Fig. 5.—Young of *Tylenchus radicicola*, after entering a root.

s, spear; *b*, sucking-bulb; *p*, ventral excretory pore; *i*, intestine; *n*, unicellular ventral gland; *u*, anus.

Fig. 6.—Immature *Tylenchus radicicola* shedding its skin.

c, the old skin being cast off; *s*, the old and the new spear; *p*, the ventral excretory pore; *v*, the unicellular ventral gland; *o*, rudimentary sexual organs.

suction by means of the sucking-bulb, at the same time thrusting forth its spear by means of the muscles attached to its three-bulbed base. The cells of the epidermis of the rootlet having been thus pierced are sucked dry, and at the aperture thus made other and deeper cells are similarly attacked. Continuing this line of action, the little worm makes its way into the rootlet, where its presence soon excites abnormal growth, resulting in galls, which vary in size, according to the species of plant attacked, from the size of a pin's head to that of a large walnut. In consequence of these attacks, many cultivated crops, as, for instance, potato, cabbage, banana, pea, bean, members of the melon family, beet, parsnip, radish, tomato, plum, apricot, peach, almond, grape, and many others suffer much or succumb altogether.

Fig. 7.—Neck of the worm shown in Fig. 5 more highly magnified.

s, spear; *b*, median sucking-bulb; *p*, ventral excretory pore.

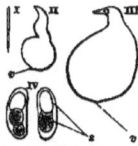

Fig. 8.—*Tylenchus radicicola.*

I, a young larva. II, a half-grown female. III, a full-grown female. IV, two eggs. *v*, the vulva; *s*, the segments of the egg after the first division. First three figures magnified twenty-five times, the others three hundred times.

The worm is a veritable pest in many parts of New South Wales, Queensland and Victoria.

Soon after the young worm loses its tail the sexual organs begin to develop. The female continues to grow stouter and finally becomes a flask-shaped sac devoid of anus and with a terminal vulva. The two-parted female sexual apparatus develops enormously, and at last almost completely fills the body-cavity, the eggs contained in it numbering several hundred. These undergo segmentation *in utero*, and are deposited (in the tissues of the attacked plant) containing already well-developed embryos.

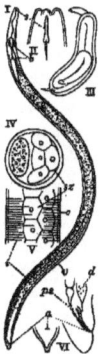

Fig. 9.—Male of *Tylenchus radicicola.*

I, male worm magnified 60 times. II, head of the same worm magnified 450 times. III, male shedding its skin for the last (?) time. IV, cross-section of the posterior part of the body. V, side view of the same part. VI, side and ventral views of the tail-end. *s*, spear; *b*, median sucking-bulb; *sz*, spermatozoa; *c*, cuticle; *i*, intestine; *v*, seminal vesicle; *d*, posterior end of the ejaculatory duct; *ps*, spicula or penes; *a*, anus.

The male worm, however, instead of continuing in the path of development followed by the female, *returns to a slender adult form*, having the following dimensions and characters :— $\frac{1\cdot}{1\cdot2}\ \frac{?}{2\cdot2}\ \frac{13\cdot}{2\cdot3}\ \frac{M}{3\cdot}\ \frac{98\cdot7}{1\cdot6}$ $1\cdot33$ mm. Cuticula with about five hundred transverse striæ; neck conoid, head truncate; lips six, distinct; spear stout; œsophageal tube one-fourth as wide as the neck, lined with thick glistening chitin; median bulb ellipsoidal, two-fifths as wide as the neck, with a large distinct chitinous central part; intestine two-thirds as wide as the body, its cells closely packed with granules; rectum twice as long as the anal body-diameter; tail obliquely hemispherical-conoid; anus inconspicuous; bursa none; spicula acute, linear, nearly straight, wider and fusiform in

G

the proximal half, about twice as long as the tail or considerably longer than the anal body-diameter ; no traces of accessory organs ; ejaculatory duct at least three to four times as long as the spicula ; spermatozoa large and spherical ; lateral wings or projections three, closely approximate, giving rise to four longitudinal lines when the lateral view is interpreted by the microscope.

Hab.—Roots of cabbage, potato, banana, radish, pea, peanut, cow-pea, bean, squash, pumpkin, sanfoin, melon, cucumber, tomato, beet, plum, apricot, peach, almond, fig, walnut, willow, gourd, begonia, sunflower, amaranth, dahlia, purslane, egg-plant, spinach, maize, orange, grape, mulberry, morning-glory, petunia, spiræa, buddleia, shepherd's purse, blackberry, and probably numerous other plants, New South Wales, Queensland, and Victoria.

2. **T. devastatrix,** Kühn. $\frac{9}{8}\frac{8\cdot}{16}\frac{13\cdot}{2\cdot}\frac{61\cdot}{82}\frac{93\cdot}{1\cdot2}$ 1·6 mm. The cuticle is traversed by about one thousand plain transverse striæ. The slightly convex-conoid neck termi-

nates in a truncate head, the limits of whose lip-region are not easily made out. The lips are rudimentary, and there are no papillæ, unless they be represented by exceedingly minute projections immediately round the narrow mouth-opening. The well-developed spear is moved forward by three muscles passing obliquely from the three bulbs to the outer margin of the lip-region. The muscular ellipsoidal median bulb, lying just in front of the middle of the neck, has the same width as the head ; its distinct three - chambered central cavity is thickly lined with chitin, which serves as the internal attachment of nucleated radial muscles. Somewhat behind the oblique nerve-ring the œsophageal tube begins to expand, and, continuing to do so to the end, thus forms a posterior bulb (fully one-fourth as long as the neck), which always contains about three large nuclei. These nuclei appear to me to indicate that this bulb or swelling is glandular rather than muscular in function. The intestine begins as an exceedingly fine tube leading backward from the œsophagus ; it soon becomes three-fourths as wide as the body, and appears to be made up of two rows of cells packed with coarse granules. The limits of the rectum are indefinite, but it

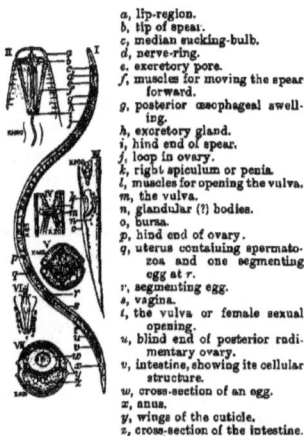

a, lip-region.
b, tip of spear.
c, median sucking-bulb.
d, nerve-ring.
e, excretory pore.
f, muscles for moving the spear forward.
g, posterior œsophageal swelling.
h, excretory gland.
i, hind end of spear.
j, loop in ovary.
k, right spiculum or penis.
l, muscles for opening the vulva.
m, the vulva.
n, glandular (?) bodies.
o, bursa.
p, hind end of ovary.
q, uterus containing spermatozoa and one segmenting egg at r.
r, segmenting egg.
s, vagina.
t, the vulva or female sexual opening.
u, blind end of posterior rudimentary ovary.
v, intestine, showing its cellular structure.
w, cross-section of an egg.
x, anus.
y, wings of the cuticle.
z, cross-section of the intestine.

FIG. 9.—Side view of the devastating eel-worm.

I, a female worm. II, head of the same worm more highly magnified. III, tail of a male. IV, view from below, of the female sexual opening. V, cross-section of the worm passing through the sucking-bulb. VI, front view of the penes and their accessory parts. VII, cross-section through the middle of a female, showing how the body cavity is filled completely by the ovary (w) and the intestine (z).

is not more than half as long as the anal body-diameter. The unicellular ventral gland lies just behind the œsophagus, and empties, by means of a slender tube devoid of an ampulla, through the ventral excretory pore, situated half-way between the nerve-ring and the posterior end of the œsophagus. The distance between the two lateral wings is equal to one-fourth the length of the diameter of the body. The median fields are very narrow ; no submedian fields came under notice. The tail is conoid from the conspicuously-projecting vulva. The anus is inconspicuous. There are no anal glands. The vulva, a transverse slit one-half as long as the body is wide, is opened during copulation and oviposition by means of four pairs of oblique muscles arranged in two antagonistic groups, one anterior to the vulva and the other posterior. Each of the posterior pairs is attached distally near the ends of the slit and proximally to the body wall near the ventral submedian lines some distance back from the vulva. The antagonistic muscles are arranged similarly, but in front of the vulva. The short vagina leads forward into the uterus, which is as long as the distance from the vulva to the anus, and in adult worms commonly contains one or two eggs (three-fourths as wide as the body and twice as long as wide), which are in the later stages of segmentation. The anterior part of the uterus is occupied by numerous spermatozoa, which are placed there by copulation with a male, and which fertilise the egg immediately on its entry into the uterus. A rudimentary sac-like posterior branch of the sexual organ extends backward from the vulva half-way to the anus. The females are viviparous or ovoviviparous. $\frac{9}{9} \frac{8^{\cdot}}{17} \frac{12^{\cdot}}{19} \frac{-31}{9} \frac{93^{\cdot}}{14}$ 1·4 mm. In the male the anus projects so as to be prominent. The transparent ribless bursa originates anteriorly opposite the proximal ends of the spicula, and ends behind the middle of the tail or near its end. The two equal elongated arcuate-cuneiform spicula are one and one-half times longer than the anal body-diameter, their proximæ being slightly cephaloid by expansion. The thin and inconspicuous accessory pieces, in which the spicula slide, are half as long as the spicula. In the neighbourhood of each spiculum and behind the anus I observed cells which may be glandular in function. The single testicle extends forward to near the œsophagus. The ripe spermatozoa are one-sixth as wide as the body.

Syn.—*T. dipsaci*, Kühn ; *T. allii*, Beyerinck ; *T. hyacinthi*, Prilleux ; *T. Haversteinii*, Kühn.

Hab.—Parasitic in onions, hyacinths, teasel, rye, oats, buck-wheat, clover, potatoes, &c.

3. **T. granulosus**, n.sp. $\frac{2\cdot8}{2\cdot3} \frac{10^{\cdot}}{2\cdot7} \frac{16^{\cdot}}{2\cdot8} \frac{56^{\cdot}}{3\cdot3} \frac{90^{\cdot}}{2\cdot4}$ ·68 mm. The cuticle is traversed by about four hundred and seventy-five transverse striæ, which exist in the outer as well as the inner layers. The conoid neck terminates anteriorly in a head somewhat rounded in front and bearing six somewhat spherical lips. The stout spear is one-tenth as

wide as the head, and the three bulbs at its base form a triple knot three times as wide as the shaft. Anteriorly the œsophagus is one-fourth as wide as the neck; somewhat behind the middle of the neck it expands to form a muscular prolate bulb one-half as wide as the neck. Thence it passes through the oblique nerve-ring situated just behind the bulb, and from being there one-fifth as wide as the neck it becomes rather suddenly one-half as wide as the neck, and joins the intestine in a rather indefinite manner at 16%, as stated in the formula. The ventral excretory pore is situated at a distance behind the median bulb equal to thrice the length of that organ. The intestine is composed of cells containing coarse granules. The distance between the wings of the cuticle equals one-third the width of the body. The tail is conoid to near the terminus, where it diminishes suddenly to a blunt point. I saw only immature females, and cannot give details concerning the sexual organs. The above formula is the average of four specimens. Male unknown.

Hab.—Observed in numbers in brown rotten cavities three-fourths of an inch deep in the root-stock of banana plants, and also occasionally among the outer sheaths of the plants as well as in the adjacent soil, Fiji, 1891.

4. **T. similis,** n.sp. ——————— Nearly all the information I have with regard to this species is set forth in the sketches on Pl. VII.

Hab.—Found about diseased banana plants, Fiji, July, 1891.

5. **T. multicinctus,** n.sp. $\frac{5 \cdot \quad 16 \cdot \quad 7 \quad 66 \cdot \quad 97 \cdot}{29 \quad 35 \quad 7 \quad 48 \quad 24}$ ·5 mm. Cuticula traversed by numerous plain transverse striæ, which are displayed in the outer as well as the inner layers; neck conoid; head somewhat rounded and presenting six transparent lips; spear well developed, stout, and with three prominent bulbs, in action guided by well-developed chitinous processes behind the lips; anterior part of the œsophagus a chitinous tube; median sucking-bulb considerably behind the middle of the œsophagus, ellipsoidal and presenting a well developed internal valve; nerve-ring oblique, close behind the median bulb; posterior part of the œsophagus at first tubular, but finally expanding into a swelling nearly half as wide as the base of the neck; intestine granular, two-thirds as wide as the body; tail convex-conoid, blunt; nature of the female sexual organs unknown. $\frac{5 \cdot \quad 15 \cdot \quad 22 \cdot \quad -M \quad 97 \cdot}{29 \quad 34 \quad 35 \quad 4 \cdot \quad 23}$ ·5 mm. Spicula two, equal, elongate, tapering, acute, arcuate, proximal ends not cephalated, one and one-half times as long as the anal body-diameter; tail completely enveloped in the striated bursa which springs from opposite the proximal ends of the spicula and reaches its greatest development opposite the anus; accessory pieces half as long as the spicula and placed parallel to them. The worm is well figured on Pl. VII.

Hab.—Found about the roots of banana plants, Fiji, July, 1891.

Genus APHELENCHUS, Bastian.

Transparent striated round worms, nearly always totally devoid of bristles or setæ, varying in length from one-half a millimetre to one and a-half millimetres, attacking the tissues of plants by means of a spear and sucking apparatus of the following construction : a more or less distinctly three-bulbed spear, capable of being thrust forth and withdrawn by appropriate muscles, is connected with a powerful œsophageal sucking-bulb, by means of a tube whose lining is more chitinous than is usual in most Nematode genera. Behind the median bulb, the œsophagus continues for a short distance as a narrow tube, but soon gradually enlarges and joins the intestine in such a manner that it is often impossible to say where the œsophagus leaves off and the intestine begins. The oblique nerve-ring is situated just behind the sucking-bulb.

1. **A. microlaimus,** Cobb. $\frac{6\ 4\cdot91\ 10\cdot3\ -60\ \frac{45}{8\cdot2}\ 95\cdot3}{7\ 13\ 17\ 1}$ $\cdot7$ mm. The cuticula is traversed by seven hundred transverse striæ. To the slightly convex-conoid neck succeeds a somewhat rounded head with six minute rudimentary lips, which are to be seen only in certain oblique aspects, and which are destitute of papillæ. The pharynx is armed with an unusually short spear, whose base presents three rudimentary bulbs. The œsophagus is one-fourth as wide as the neck and terminates posteriorly in an ellipsoidal bulb four-fifths as wide as the base of the neck ; thence the alimentary canal continues, at first narrow, but gradually widening. The bulb is, morphologically, probably the median bulb—the posterior part of the œsophagus being rudimentary and indistinguishable from the intestine. Nervefibres appear to exist both behind and in front of the bulb. The rectum seems to be about equal in length to the anal body-diameter. The ventral excretory pore is situated at a distance behind the œsophageal bulb equal to twice the length of the latter organ ; the gland of which it is the outlet is a very long and narrow cell as far behind the excretory pore as the latter is behind the mouth. The tail is conical to the terminus, which forms an outlet for the secretions of the caudal glands. The posterior branch of the sexual organs is only half as long as the anterior, and is therefore somewhat rudimentary. $\frac{\cdot9\ 1\ 10\cdot5\ -M^{66}\ 95\cdot1}{8\ 13\ 17\ 2\cdot4\ 17}$ $\cdot66$ mm. The ventrally-arcuate conoid tail of the male presents a

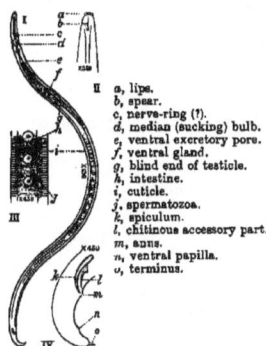

a, lips.
b, spear.
c, nerve-ring (?).
d, median (sucking) bulb.
e, ventral excretory pore.
f, ventral gland.
g, blind end of testicle.
h, intestine.
i, cuticle.
j, spermatozoa.
k, spiculum.
l, chitinous accessory part.
m, anus.
n, ventral papilla.
o, terminus.

Fig. 10.—*Aphelenchus microlaimus.*
I, male worm. II, head of the same. III, portion of the middle of the body. IV, posterior extremity.

single median ventral papilla near the middle. The two linear acute spicula, half as long as the tail, are so close together that when seen in profile they appear as one. The proximal ends are not cephaloid. In front of the spicula is a structure one-half as long as the spicula themselves, concerning whose function I am uncertain. It may be accessory to the spicula, as it can be exserted at the same time. The blind end of the testicle is sometimes reflexed, and in it commences the development of the spermatozoa, which are arranged in single file through the organ.

Hab.—Common on grass, Sydney, N.S.W., Australia.

2. **A. longicaudatus,** n.sp.　$\frac{2\cdot6}{1\cdot6}\frac{11\cdot}{1\cdot9}\frac{10\cdot}{1\cdot6}\frac{-55\cdot^{40}}{2\cdot2}\frac{70\cdot}{1\cdot1}$ ·8 mm.　Cuticle apparently without markings; hairs none; neck conoid; cephalic setæ none; head truncate, the lip-region transparent; lips obscure, probably six; spear acute, slender, with inconspicuous posterior ending; œsophagus one-third to one-half as wide as the neck; bulb one-half to two-thirds as wide as the neck, twice as long as wide, or more, with a refracting chitinous central part; tail conical, in its posterior half setaceous; vulva inconspicuous; uterus with possibly a rudimentary posterior branch; eggs twice as long as the body is wide and one-third as wide as long, probably deposited before segmentation begins. $\frac{3\cdot}{1\cdot4}\frac{14\cdot}{2\cdot}\frac{13\cdot}{2\cdot}\frac{-M}{2\cdot6}\frac{72\cdot}{1\cdot}$ ·57 mm.　The male tail is like that of the female in form. There is no bursa or papilla or supplementary organ of any kind. The arcuate-cuneiform spicula are a little longer than the anal body-diameter, their proximal ends not being cephaloid. There is a chitinous structure in front of the spicula, possibly the chitinous terminal portion of the combined rectum and sexual opening, which is half as long as the spicula and expanded proximally much as in *A. microlaimus.* Figured on Pl. vii.

Hab.—Soil about banana plants, Fiji, July, 1891. Not common.

3. **A. minor,** n.sp.　$\frac{4}{8}\frac{7}{7}\frac{12\cdot}{2\cdot9}\frac{-68\cdot}{2\cdot6}\frac{92\cdot}{1\cdot4}$ ·48 mm.　Cuticle naked as usual, and with very fine markings, if any. The conoid neck ends in a truncate head with a definite lip-region. I am uncertain about the details of the pharynx. The prolate bulb contains a distinct valvular structure. The œsophageal tube is heavily lined with chitin. The intestine is coarsely granular. The ventral pore is situated somewhat behind the sucking-bulb. The conoid tail ends in what appears to be a conical outlet for the secretions of the caudal glands. The vulva is inconspicuous. The eggs are one-half as wide as the body and over twice as long as wide. Figured on Pl. iii.

Hab.—Found about the roots of banana plants, Fiji.

EXPLANATION OF PLATES.

Plate I.

Mononchus digiturus.

Fig. 1. Female worm. Fig. 2. Terminus of the tail. Fig. 3. Neck and head. Fig. 4. Tail.

a, spinneret; b, mouth-opening; c, papillæ; d, pharynx; e, two submedian teeth; f, single dorsal tooth; g, nerve-ring; h, œsophagus; i, vulva; j, anus; k, intestine; l, cardiac constriction.

Mononchus gymnolaimus.

Fig. 1. Female worm. Fig. 2. Head of the same worm more highly magnified. Fig. 3. Anal region.

a, papillæ round the mouth; b, papillæ on the margin of the head; c, rectum; d, lateral organ; e, striæ on wall of the pharynx; f, muscles of the pharynx; g, œsophagus; h, caudal glands; i, dorsal tooth; j, œsophagus; k, intestine; l, vulva and vagina; m, ovum, flexure in ovary; n, anus; o, excretory pore (?); p, cardiac collum; q, œsophagus.

Mononchus minor.

Fig. 1. Female worm. Fig. 2. Head of the same worm more highly magnified. Fig. 3. Neck and head. Fig. 4. Tail. Fig. 5. Portion of body.

a, papillæ on the margin of the head; b, papillæ round the mouth; c, dorsal tooth; d, rasp-like teeth on wall of the pharynx; e, beginning of the œsophagus; f, nerve-ring; g, anus; h, lateral field; i, vulva; j, egg; k, œsophagus.

Rhabditis filiformis (?).

Fig. 1. Female worm. Fig. 2. Head. Fig. 3. Head. Fig. 4. Portion of the body.

a, pharynx; b, beginning of the œsophagus; c, œsophagus; d, cardiac bulb; e, flexure in ovary; f, blind end of ovary; g, vulva; h, blind end of ovary; i, posterior end of pharynx; j, anus; k, flexure in intestine; l, egg.

Plate II.

Aulolaimus exilis.

Fig. 1. A female worm. Fig. 2. Head of the same worm. Fig. 3. Neck. Fig. 4. Cardiac region.

a, lips; b, pharynx; c, nerve-ring; d, base of pharynx; e, vulva; f, anus; g, œsophagus; h, cardiac bulb; i, cardiac bulb; j, beginning of the intestine.

Chromadora minima.

Fig. 1. Neck. Fig. 2. Female worm.

a, cephalic setæ; b, pharynx; c, lateral organ; d, œsophagus; e, cardiac swelling; f, intestine; g, cardiac collum; h, vulva; i, anus; j, spinneret.

Monhystera rustica.

Fig. 1. Female worm. Fig. 2. Head and neck of the same worm.

a, cardiac collum; b, intestine: c, blind end of ovary; d, egg; e, vulva; f, anus; g, cephalic setæ; h, base of the pharynx; i, lateral organ; j, cardiac collum.

Dorylaimus labyrinthostoma.

Fig. 1. A female worm. Fig. 2. Head of the same worm more highly magnified. Fig. 3. Part of the neck.

a, mouth-opening; b, one of the inner row of papillæ; c, one of the outer row of papillæ; d, row of rasping (?) organs; e, spear-guide; f, base of the spear; g, cardiac collum; h, vulva; i, pre-rectum; j, anus; k, nerve-ring; l, œsophagus.

Chromadora musæ.

Fig. 1. An immature female worm. Fig. 2. Terminus of the tail. Fig. 3. Head.

a, cardiac bulb; b, nerve-ring; c, lateral organ; d, dorsal tooth; e, base of the pharynx; f, anus; g, œsophagus.

Plate III.

Young Rhabditis.

Fig. 1. Young worm. Fig. 2. Head and neck. Fig. 3. Head.

a, lips; b, pharynx; c, œsophagus; d, median bulb; e, nerve-ring; f, cardiac bulb; g, anus; h, nerve-ring.

Aphelenchus minor.

Fig. 1. Anterior part of a female worm. Fig. 2. Tail. Fig. 3. Posterior part of a female worm.

a, tubular part of the œsophagus; b, median sucking-bulb; c, excretory pore; d, vulva; e, vulva; f, anus; g, spinneret.

Rhabditis coronata.

Fig. 1. A female worm. Fig. 2. Head of the same worm more highly magnified.

a, lips; b, pharynx; c, median bulb; d, nerve-ring; e, cardiac bulb; f, cardiac collum; g, intestine; h, egg; i, vulva; j, egg; k, anus.

RHABDITIS MONHYSTERA.

Fig. 1. Female worm. Fig. 2. Male worm. Fig. 3. Tail of a male. Fig. 4. Head. Fig. 5. Tail of a female. Fig. 6. An egg with embryo.

a, blind end of ovary ; *b*, egg ; *c*, vulva ; *d*, egg ; *e*, flexure in ovary ; *f*, anus ; *g*, ductus ejaculatorius ; *h*, spiculum ; *i*, anterior group, ribs of bursa ; *j*, median group, ribs of bursa ; *k*, posterior group, ribs of bursa ; *l*, pharynx ; *m*, œsophagus ; *n*, median bulb ; *o*, nerve-ring ; *p*, excretory pore ; *q*, cardiac bulb ; *r*, intestine ; *s*, flexure in testicle ; *t*, vas deferens ; *u*, papillæ on lips ; *v*, pharynx ; *w*, rectum ; *x*, lateral pores on tail of female ; *y*, embryo.

RHABDITIS PELLIOIDES.

Fig. 1. A female worm. Fig. 2. Head. Fig. 3. Tail. Fig. 4. Small portion of the body. Fig. 5. Neck and head. Fig. 6. Tail of a male. Fig. 7. Tail of a male.

a, lips ; *b*, pharynx ; *c*, median bulb ; *d*, nerve-ring ; *e*, cardiac bulb ; *f*, pharynx ; *g*, papillæ ; *h*, lip ; *i*, anus ; *j*, lateral wings ; *k*, flexure in ovary ; *l*, blind end of testicle ; *m*, ribs of bursa ; *n*, spermatozoa ; *o*, bursa ; *p*, egg ; *q*, ribs of bursa ; *r*, ribs of bursa ; *s*, egg ; *t*, vulva ; *u*, anus ; *v*, median bulb ; *w*, ribs of bursa ; *x*, excretory pore ; *y*, ribs of bursa ; *z*, ribs of bursa.

PLATE IV.

TRIPYLA MINOR.

Fig. 1. Female worm. Fig. 2. Head of the same worm more highly magnified. Fig. 3. Tail of a female. Fig. 4. Tail of a female. Fig. 5. Tail of a female. Fig. 6. Front view of head. Fig. 7. Spinneret in the terminus of the tail. (Figs. 3, 4, 5 show difference in form and amount of motion.)

a, one of the papillæ round the mouth ; *b*, one of the lateral setæ ; *c*, one of the submedian setæ ; *d*, supposed lateral organ ; *e*, anus ; *f*, spinneret opening ; *g*, anus ; *h*, anus ; *i*, nerve-ring ; *j*, cardiac collum ; *k*, egg ; *l*, vulva ; *m*, lateral seta ; *n*, one of the pairs of submedian setæ ; *o*, anus ; *p*, pharynx.

PRISMATOLAIMUS INTERMEDIUS.

Fig. 1. Female worm. Fig. 2. Head of the same worm more highly magnified. Fig. 3. Cardiac region showing structures (?) of unknown significance. Fig. 4. Portion of the female near the vulva. Fig. 5. Anal region. Fig. 6. Tail. Fig. 7. Terminus of tail. Fig. 8. Portion of body drawn to show striations and intestine.

a, cephalic setæ ; *b*, pharynx ; *c*, œsophagus ; *d*, ovum ; *e*, rectum ; *f*, vulva ; *g*, anus ; *h*, posterior end of the œsophagus ; *i*, structures of unknown significance ; *j*, beginning of the intestine ; *k*, blind end of ovary ; *l*, vulva ; *m*, terminus.

DIPLOGASTER PARVUS and MINOR.

Fig. 1. Female worm. Fig. 2. Neck and head of another worm. Fig. 3. Head of female shown in Fig. 1. Fig. 4. Side view of body. Fig. 5. Anal region of a male.

a, pharynx ; *b*, dorsal tooth ; *c*, lateral field ; *d*, median bulb ; *e*, lips ; *f*, dorsal tooth ; *g*, pharynx ; *h*, cardiac bulb ; *i*, flexure of the ovary ; *j*, blind end of ovary ; *k*, vulva ; *l*, anus ; *m*, median bulb ; *n*, nerve-ring ; *o*, cardiac bulb ; *p*, intestine ; *q*, male papilla ; *r*, male papilla ; *s*, male papilla ; *t*, male papilla ; *u*, male papilla ; *v*, left spiculum ; *w*, accessory piece.

H

CEPHALOBUS INFESTANS.

Fig. 1. Male worm. Fig. 2. Tail of same worm more highly magnified. Fig. 3. Anal region of a male. Fig. 4. Neck and head.

     a, male papilla ; *b*, male papilla ; *c*, male papilla ; *d*, male papilla ; *e*, left spiculum ; *f*, accessory piece ; *g*, lips ; *h*, base of the pharynx ; *i*, nerve-ring ; *j*, cardiac bulb ; *k*, intestine ; *l*, flexure in testicle.

PLATE V.

DORYLAIMUS EXILIS.

Fig. 1. A female worm. Fig. 2. Tail of the same worm more highly magnified. Fig. 3. Cardiac region. Fig. 4. Head. Fig. 5. An egg.

     a, pre-rectum ; *b*, rectum ; *c*, anus ; *d*, lips ; *e*, spear ; *f*, nerve-ring ; *g*, vulva ; *h*, œsophagus ; *i*, beginning of the intestine.

DORYLAIMUS GRANULIFERUS.

Fig. 1. A female worm. Fig. 2. Tail. Fig. 3. Cardiac region. Fig. 4. Head. Fig. 5. Portion of the body.

     a, tip of the spear ; *b*, papilla of the inner row ; *c*, papilla of the outer row ; *d*, papilla of the outer row ; *e*, intestine ; *f*, lateral field ; *g*, nerve-ring ; *h*, cardiac collum ; *i*, flexure in anterior ovary ; *j*, egg ; *k*, vulva ; *l*, blind end posterior ovary ; *m*, pre-rectum ; *n*, anus ; *o*, œsophagus near posterior end ; *p*, beginning of intestine ; *q*, rectum ; *r*, anus.

DORYLAIMUS OBTUSUS.

Fig. 1. Young female worm. Fig. 2. Tail. Fig. 3. Head and anterior part of the neck. Fig. 4. Tail. Fig. 5. Head.

     a, spear ; *b*, lips ; *c*, pre-rectum ; *d*, anus ; *e*, intestine ; *f*, pre-rectum ; *g*, anus ; *h*, nerve-ring ; *i*, nerve-ring ; *j*, immature female sexual organs ; *k*, anus ; *l*, œsophagus.

DORYLAIMUS PERFECTUS (?).

Fig. 1. Female worm. Fig. 2. Head and neck of the same worm. Fig. 3. Tail. Fig. 4. Head.

     a, tip of the spear ; *b*, one of the inner row of papillæ ; *c*, one of the outer row of papillæ ; *d*, base of the lips ; *e*, nerve-ring ; *f*, intestine ; *g*, pre-rectum ; *h*, egg ; *i*, vulva ; *j*, anus.

PLATE VI.

DORYLAIMUS PERFECTUS.

Fig. 1. Male worm. Fig. 2. Anterior part of the neck of the same worm. Fig. 3. Tail end of the male shown in Fig. 1. Fig. 4. Anal region. Fig. 5. Spiculum. Fig. 6. Portion of intestine.

     a, nerve-ring ; *b*, œsophagus ; *c*, intestine ; *d*, intestine ; *e*, blind end of anterior testicle ; *f*, pre-rectum ; *g*, left spiculum ; *h*, anus ; *i*, blind end of posterior testicle ; *j*, anus ; *k*, papillæ ; *l*, junction of the testicles ; *m*, spear ; *n*, guiding-collar for spear ; *o*, intestine ; *p*, ventral row male papillæ ; *q*, pore ; *r*, papillæ ; *s*, gland ; *t*, nerve-ring ; *u*, spiculum ; *v*, oblique copulatory muscles ; *w*, oblique copulatory muscles ; *x*, œsophagus where it enlarges ; *y*, tessellation of the intestine ; *z*, a spiculum.

Dorylaimus longicollis.

Fig. 1. A young worm. Fig. 2. Female, nearly adult. Fig. 3. Head and anterior part of the neck. Fig. 4. Tail. Fig. 5. Vulva and vagina. Fig. 6. Portion of the body.

a, nerve-ring; b, œsophagus; c, anus; d, anus; e, blind end of ovary; f, vulva; g, nerve-ring; h, cardiac collum; i, anus; j, pre-rectum; k, intestine; l, lateral field; m, vagina; n, vulva; o, lips; p, spear; q, nerve-ring; r, œsophagus where it enlarges.

Plate VII.

Aphelenchus longicaudatus.

Fig. 1. A female worm. Fig. 2. Anal region of a male. Fig. 3. Head and neck. Fig. 4. Region of the vulva.

a, lips; b, base of spear; c, bulb; d, excretory pore; e, bulb; f, excretory pore; g, nerve-ring; h, right spiculum; i, accessory organ; j, anus; k, egg; l, vulva; m, anus; n, egg; o, vulva.

Tylenchus similis.

Fig. 1. Head and neck. Fig. 2. Portion of the body. Fig. 3. Tail of a male. Fig. 4. Male worm. Fig. 5. Anal region of a male.

a, spear; b, bulb; c, excretory pore; d, striæ; e, intestine; f, bursa; g, spicula; h, bursa; i, tips of the spicula.

Tylencholaimus ensiculiferus.

Fig. 1. Immature female. Fig. 2. Posterior part of the neck. Fig. 3. Anterior part of the neck. Fig. 4. Tail.

a, tip of the spear; b, narrow part of the shaft of spear; c, wider part of the shaft of spear; d, base of the spear; e, base of the spear; f, tube leading to bulb; g, bulb; h, intestine.

Tylenchus multicinctus.

Fig. 1. A male worm. Fig. 2. Neck and head. Fig. 3. Small portion of the body. Fig. 4. Head. Fig. 5. Tail of a male. Fig. 6. Tail of a male. Fig. 7. Tail of a female.

a, spear-guide; b, base of spear; c, chitinous tube leading to bulb; d, median bulb; e, nerve-ring; f, excretory pore; g, cardiac bulb; h, intestine; i, proximal ends of spicula; j, shaft of spiculum; k, accessory piece; l, lateral wings; m, bursa; n, anus; o, proximæ of spicula; p, points of spicula; q, bursa.

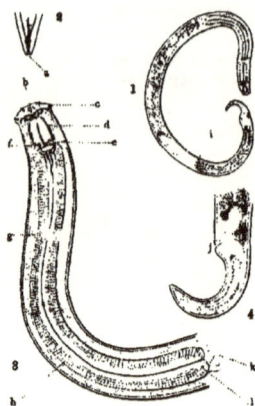

Mononchus digiturus, n. sp.

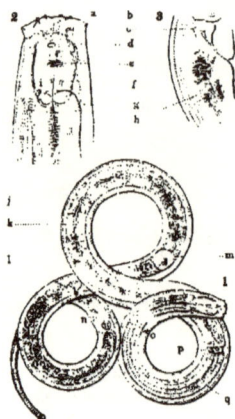

Mononchus gymnolaimus, n. sp.

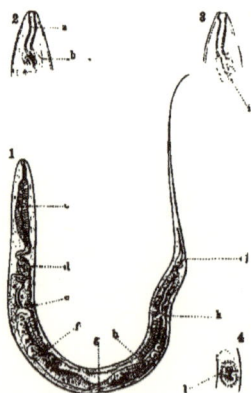

Rhabditis filiformis (?), B'ts'li.

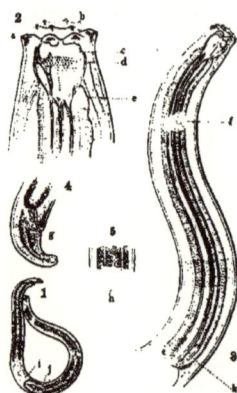

Mononchus minor, n. sp.

Nematodes; Banana-plants, Fiji.

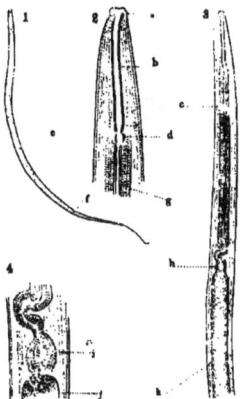

Aulolaimus axilis, n. sp.

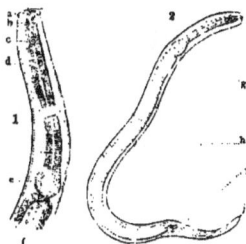

Chromadora minima, n. sp.

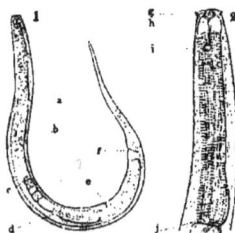

Monhystera rustica, B'ts'ti.

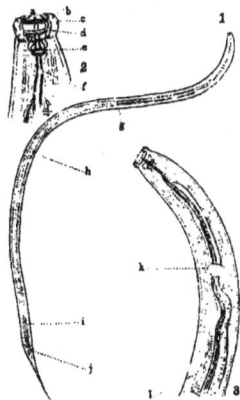

Dorylaimus labyrinthostomus, n. sp.

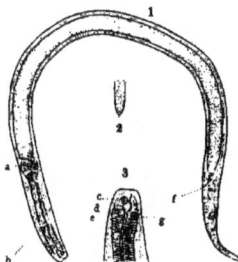

Chromadora Musae, n. sp.

Nematodes; Banana-plants, Fiji.

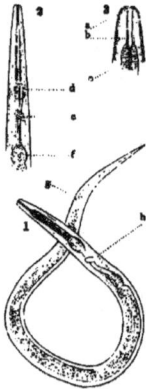

Young Rhabditis, sp. (?)

Aphelenchus minor, n. sp.

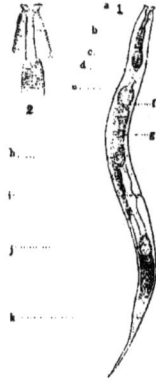

Rhabditis coronata, n. sp.

Rhabditis pellioides, B'ts'li.

Rhabditis monhystera, B'ts'li.

Nematodes; Banana-plants, Fiji.

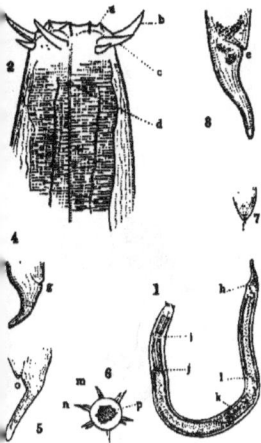

Tripyla minor, n. sp.

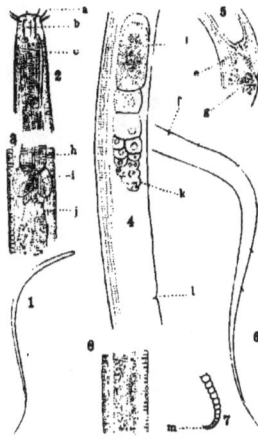

Prismatoluimus intermedius (?), B'ts'li.

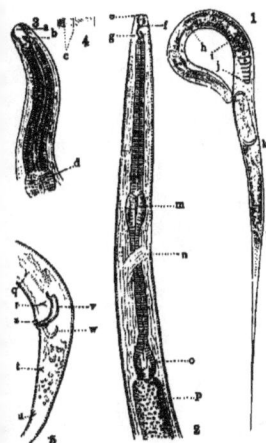

Figs. 2 and 5 Diplogaster parvus, n. sp.
Figs. 1, 3 and 4 Diplogaster minor, n. sp.

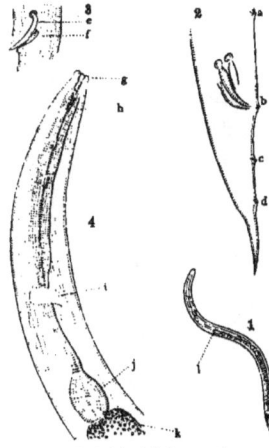

Cephalobus infestans, n. sp.

Nematodes; Banana-plants, Fiji.

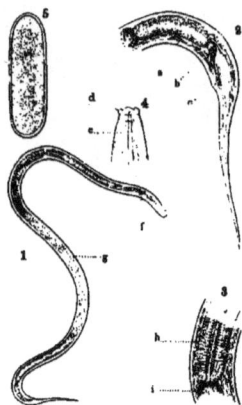

Dorylaimus exilis, n. sp.

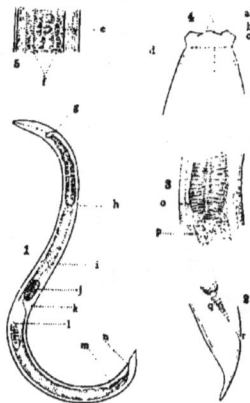

Dorylaimus granuliferus, n. sp.

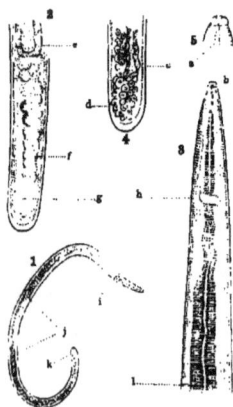

Dorylaimus obtusus, n. sp.

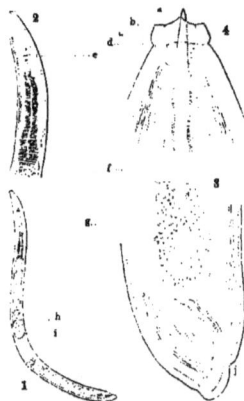

Dorylaimus perfectus (?), n. sp.

Nematodes; Banana-plants, Fiji.

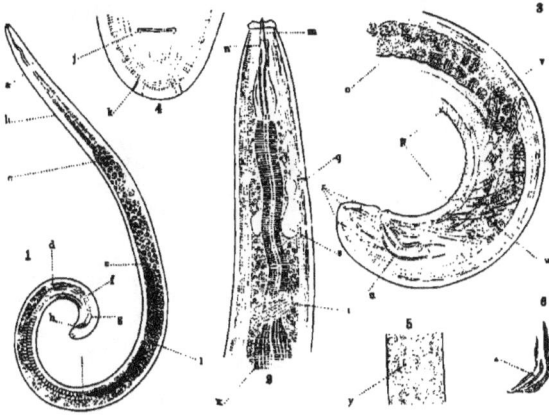

Dorylaimus perfectus, n. sp.

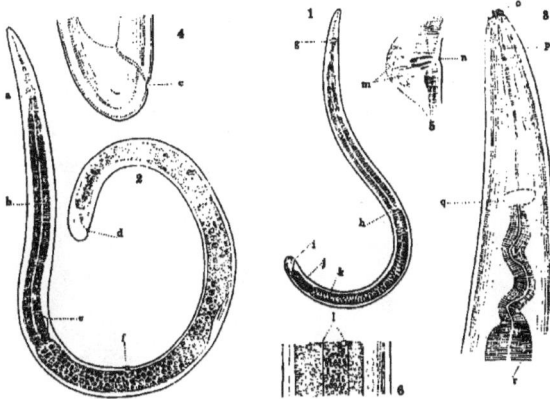

Dorylaimus longicollis, n. sp.

Nematodes; Banana-plants, Fiji.

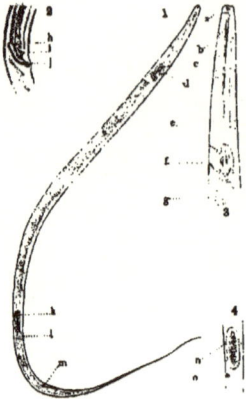

Aphelenchus longicaudatus, n. sp.

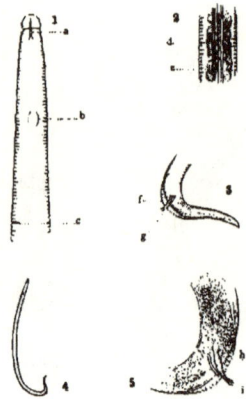

Tylenchus similis, n. sp.

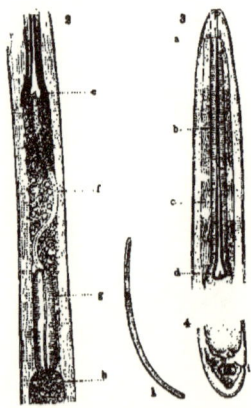

Tylencholaimus ansiciliferus, n. sp.

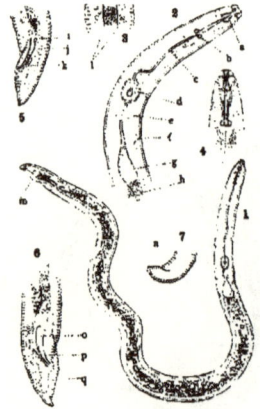

Tylenchus multicinctus, n. sp.

Nematodes; Banana-plants, Fiji.